BETTER HOMES AND GARDENS®

Quick, Healthy and Delicious Cooking

BETTER HOMES AND GARDENS® BOOKS

Des Moines

WECARE!

All of us at Better Homes and Gardens® Books are dedicated to providing you with the information and ideas you need to create tasty foods. We welcome your comments and suggestions. Write us at: Better Homes and Gardens® Books, Cookbook Editorial Department, RW-240, 1716 Locust St., Des Moines, IA 50309-3023

If you would like to order additional copies of any of our books, call 1-800-678-2803 or check with your local bookstore.

Our seal assures you that every recipe in *Quick, Healthy and Delicious Cooking* has been tested in the Better Homes and Gardens® Test Kitchen. This means that each recipe is practical and reliable, and meets our high standards of taste appeal. We guarantee your satisfaction with this book for as long as you own it.

BETTER HOMES AND GARDENS® BOOKS
An Imprint of Meredith® Books
President, Book Group: Joseph J. Ward
Vice President and Editorial Director: Elizabeth P. Rice
Executive Editor: Connie Schrader
Art Director: Ernest Shelton
Art Production: Randall Yontz
Graphic Production Coordinator: Paula Forest
Test Kitchen Director: Sharon Stilwell

Quick, Healthy and Delicious Cooking
Editor: Mary Major Williams
Writers: Nancy Wall Hopkins, Marge Steenson, Linda Foley Woodrum
Graphic Designer: Lynda Haupert
Test Kitchen Product Supervisor: Marilyn Cornelius
Food Stylists: Lynn Blanchard, Janet Pittman, Jennifer Peterson
Photographer: Mike Dieter

On the cover: Chicken with Mushroom-Peppercorn Sauce (page 12)

Meredith Corporation Corporate Officers:
Chairman of the Executive Committee: E. T. Meredith III
Chairman of the Board, President and Chief Executive Officer: Jack D. Rehm
Group Presidents: Joseph J. Ward, Books; William T. Kerr, Magazines; Philip A. Jones, Broadcasting; Allen L. Sabbag, Real Estate
Vice Presidents: Leo R. Armatis, Corporate Relations; Thomas G. Fisher, General Counsel and Secretary; Larry D. Hartsook, Finance; Michael A. Sell, Treasurer; Kathleen J. Zehr, Controller and Assistant Secretary

INTRODUCTION

If you are like most of today's cooks, you have less time than ever before for preparing delicious meals for your family. Yet food has never been more important. With less available time for cooking, we are realizing the importance of consuming a nutritionally balanced diet with an eye toward keeping fat, cholesterol, and sodium at healthy levels.

To meet your needs we have packed these pages with over 160 recipes that can be made in 45 minutes or less. Every recipe also fits into a healthy diet for you, your spouse, and your children. And above all, the food produced from each recipe tastes good because along with providing your bodies with the necessary nutrients in the proper amounts, food must also offer the pleasure of good taste.

If you have picked up this book, you are interested in healthy cooking. Maybe your doctor has advised someone in your family to modify their diet because of a weight problem, coronary heart disease, or high blood pressure. Or, maybe you decided on your own you wanted to prepare healthier meals for you and your family. For whatever reason you selected this book, these recipes will provide wonderful meals that the entire family will relish for years to come.

CONTENTS

QUICK AND HEALTHY KITCHEN TIPS

Where to Begin

A healthy eating plan must have dietary goals. Do you want to lose weight? Or, are you interested in reducing the fat and saturated fat in your diet? Or, would you just like to consume a generally more healthy diet? Fortunately, many of these goals overlap. By reducing fat, you will reduce calories and achieve an overall more healthy eating pattern.

Any healthy diet must include a reasonable amount of calories, fat, saturated fat, cholesterol, and sodium. Although you do not need to keep a running tally of each of these every time you take a bite of food, it's a good idea to initially do some calculations so you know where you stand and where your diet needs improvement.

Calories

The first step in designing your healthy eating plan is to establish the approximate number of calories you should consume each day. Most moderately active people need about 15 calories per pound to maintain their weight. For example, to keep from gaining or losing weight, a 133-pound woman needs 15 calories times her weight of 133 pounds or 1,995 calories per day.

When you consume more calories than you body burns, you gain weight. And when you consume fewer calories you lose weight. And when your caloric intake equals your caloric expenditure, your weight remains the same.

A pound of body fat contains about 3,500 calories, about the same as in a pound of butter. So figure the arithmetic of reducing this way: Eat 3,500 fewer calories than your body uses and shed 1 pound of body fat. Take in 7,000 fewer calories and lose 2 pounds.

What does this mean for everyday living? By consuming 1,000 fewer calories per day than you burn up, you should lose about 2 pounds in a week. Or, cut 500 calories per day and lose 1 pound per week. You can do this by consuming fewer calories, burning more calories or doing both.

Remember you can burn additional calories by increasing the amount of exercise you do each day. A moderate 30-minute walk burns about 100 calories. Keep it up every day for five weeks, and subtract 3,500 calories—the equivalent of one pound of body fat.

Fat and Saturated Fat

Once you have established the amount of calories that you need to consume to maintain, lose, or gain weight, you can determine the amount of fat and saturated fat that is best for you.

Most public health organizations recommend a diet that contains no more than 30 percent calories from fat. Also, less than 10 percent of your total calories should come from saturated fat.

Since most food labels and the nutrition analyses of recipes in this book list total fat and saturated fat in grams, it's easier to simply add up grams of fat than to calculate percentages. In the beginning, you may want to write down the number of grams of fat you consume, but before long you'll keep a running tally in your head.

To figure out how much fat you should consume, first determine what 30 percent of the total calories you eat in a day equals. Here's how: If you eat 1,800 calories a day, multiply 1,800 by .30 (30 percent). You could consume 540 calories from fat. To translate this into grams, divide 540 by 9 (the number of calories in a gram of fat) to equal 60 grams. This is the number of grams of fat you should limit yourself to per day.

The same formula works for staturated fat: 1,800 times .10 (10 percent) equals 180 calories from fat. Dividing 180 by 9 equals 20 grams of saturated fat.

Don't worry about meeting the 30 percent calories from fat guideline in every food you eat, at every meal, or even in a single day. Aim for a balance of 30 percent calories from fat over two or three days. If you indulge in fried chicken, mashed potatoes and gravy, and chocolate cake one night, just try to balance it out by eating low-fat foods the following day.

Cholesterol

In addition to the cholesterol we consume in our diets, our bodies produce this waxy fatlike substance that helps form cell membranes, builds nerve sheaths, and serves as the raw material for hormone production. Unfortunately, our bodies produce almost all of the cholesterol we need, so most of what we take in our diets is excess. Excess cholesterol accumulates on blood vessel walls, clogs the vessels and may lead to coronary heart disease in some individuals.

Regardless of the amount of calories you consume, most public health organizations recommend no more than 300 milligrams of cholesterol a day.

Sodium

You need some sodium in your diet to help maintain the balance of fluids that help nutrients pass into your cells and wastes pass out. For adults consuming 1,100 to 3,300 milligrams of sodium daily is considered adequate. Many Americans consume two to three times that amount. A teaspoon of salt contains 2,000 milligrams of sodium, so it's easy to exceed the limit.

Consuming too much sodium is a health risk for those with high blood pressure, a condition affecting one in four adults. If you have a family history of high blood pressure, you should consider cutting down on sodium.

Dietary Goals

In setting dietary goals for you and your family, a good place to start is with the Dietary Guidelines for Americans established by the United States Department of Agriculture and the U. S. Department of Health and Human Services. These guidelines are:

1. Eat a variety of foods. Each day your body needs many nutrients that only a varied diet provides. Most foods have more than one nutrient, but no one food has them all.

2. Maintain a healthy weight. Being over- or underweight increases the chance of developing serious health conditions.

3. Choose a diet low in fat, saturated fat, and cholesterol. Most Americans eat more fat than they really need.

4. Choose a diet with plenty of vegetables, fruits, and grain products (breads, cereals, pasta, and rice), dry beans and peas, vegetables and fruits are sources of starch and fiber. They also are good sources of vitamins and minerals. Many of these foods also provide protein and are low in fat.

5. Use sugars only in moderation. Sugars and foods that contain sugars in large amounts provide calories, or energy, but have few other nutrients. Sugars also can contribute to tooth decay.

6. Use salt and sodium only in moderation. Sodium is an essential nutrient, but most Americans get more salt and sodium than is required. Some sodium is naturally present in food, some comes in processed foods, and some comes from salt that is added to food during cooking and at the table.

7. If you drink alcoholic beverages, do so in moderation. Alcoholic beverages are high in calories and low in nutrients. Also, drinking them is linked with many health problems and can be the cause of accidents.

Your Family's Needs

Each member of your family will have a different caloric requirement based on sex, body size, and activity level. Therefore, each member will require a different level of fat and saturated fat. The limits for sodium and cholesterol are constant for all calorie levels. Does this mean you will need to prepare different meals for each family member? Not at all. Instead your teenage son may just opt for two helpings of the main course, while you eat one. Also, those with higher calorie requirements can eat more snacks or higher calorie snacks, while someone requiring fewer calories should limit themselves to low-calorie snacks.

Children under the age of two need adequate levels of fat and calories to grow and develop normally. Do not restrict the fat and calorie levels for any children under the age of two. Older children may benefit from following the 30 percent calories from fat guideline, however, it is vitally important that they consume enough calories to meet the needs of their growing bodies.

Healthy Meal Tips

Planning healthy meals is simply putting all these facts together. *Quick, Healthy and Delicious Cooking* has done a lot of the groundwork for you. Use the recipes in this book as a basis for your meals. Refer to the nutrition analysis that follows each recipe to determine totals for calories, fat, saturated fat, cholesterol, sodium, carbohydrate, and fiber.

Here are a few more tips for planning healthy meals:

● Include lots of fruits, vegetables, grains, pasta, and breads in your meals. These foods supply the vitamins, minerals, complex carbohydrates, and dietary fiber—important nutrients that not only contribute to our overall good health, but also may help prevent certain diseases, such as heart disease and cancer.

● Limit yourself to two 3-ounce servings of meat, fish, or poultry per day.

● Be on the lookout for foods high in fat, calories, and refined sugars. Limit your servings of such foods. Their presence is obvious in such foods as butter and candy, but fats and sugar are also present in foods within other groups.

● Choose from low-fat options when available.

● Balance your diet over time, compensating for day-to-day deviations.

● Plan meals you and your family like to eat. A healthy eating pattern will never work, unless it is enjoyable to follow.

Beat the Clock

How many times have you heard someone say, "I'm too busy to be organized?" Maybe you have even said it yourself. But, planning and organization enables you to use your time and money efficiently, and will actually save more time than just about any other single step you can take in meal preparation. And, when you are just as interested in cooking healthy as in cooking quick, planning helps you get the most nutritional mileage out of your meals. Set aside some time each week to plan your meals and write out a shopping list.

Planning Meals

Planning ahead means writing down your menus for a few days or a week at a time. With some planning you won't waste precious minutes wondering what to serve and hoping you have everything. And you'll know that you're not repeating the same meal you served the day before. Using the recipes in this book, you should be able to put a meal on the table in 45 minutes or less.

Although planning requires an initial time commitment, as you do it more and more you'll find it taking less and less of your time. Once you find healthful meals that you and your family enjoy, you'll want to prepare them over and over again. You soon will become familiar with ingredients that work in your meal plan and which recipes work on the days you are most pressed for time.

Sometimes, you may find it helpful to cook more than you need and count on serving leftovers. Devise ways to use planned leftovers in salads, stir-fries, or sandwiches. Be sure to set aside the planned leftovers before serving the meal so that you're not tempted to eat more.

Use the recipes in this book, keeping your meal planning simple. Prepare only one or two recipes for each meal. Fill in the rest of the meal with plain or purchased healthful items. Easily cooked frozen vegetables or a tossed salad makes a simple addition to the menu.

Plan your meals around the main dish. Then add a variety of foods to round out the meal. Consider what the foods will look like and taste like together. Pay special attention to the fat content. If you choose a main dish that's higher in fat, choose side dishes and a dessert that contain only one or two grams of fat. If you like, add up the total grams of fat you will be consuming for each meal or the entire day. If sodium or cholesterol are a concern, you may want to tally these figures, too. Refer to the nutritional analyses that appear with each recipe and the nutrition information on package labels.

Writing a Shopping List

Write out a list before you go to the store. You will not only save time, but you will think twice about items that are not on the list and may not fit into your healthy eating patterns. Make your grocery list as you plan your menus so ingredients won't be missing when it's time to start cooking.

Make it a habit to list items when you're about to run out of them. That way you won't forget them on your next trip to the store. Keep the list on the refrigerator, and ask other family members to jot down items, they know are running low.

After you have become familiar with your favorite store, list the items you need in the order that you walk through the store. You'll avoid backtracking and the hassle of going the wrong way.

Select a store that carries all of the products you need. A one stop supermarket generally carries everything from fresh fish and meats to fresh fruits and vegetables to frozen foods. For added convenience, many stores even offer such services as dry cleaning and banking. You'll save time by not having to drive all over town for specialty food stores for individual items on your list.

Keep shopping trips to a minimum—once a week if possible. You'll save time and maybe even some money by limiting your shopping. Try to plan your shopping during the store's less busy times. For most stores that's early in the morning or late at night. Generally Saturday mornings and immediately after work are the most busy times.

Buy ingredients in the form needed in a recipe. Opt for shredded or sliced cheese, cut-up chicken; boned and skinned chicken breasts; cut-up meats, such as lean meat strips or cubes; frozen meat patties; bread crumbs and croutons; bottled minced garlic (contains some sodium), dried minced onion and garlic; parsley flakes; frozen chopped onion, green pepper, and chives; frozen fruits and vegetables; packaged cleaned spinach; coleslaw and salad mixtures; cut-up fresh vegetables; and bottled lemon juice.

Other purchases that will quickly round out meals are lower sodium canned soups and gravies, quick-cooking rice and couscous, and frozen fruits and vegetables. Remember to check the nutritional information on the label when buying any packaged food.

Reading Nutrition Labels

It is virtually impossible to buy and prepare healthy foods without reading and understanding food package labels. Recently, the laws requiring food labeling have changed in an attempt to make labels offer more complete, useful, and accurate information.

The nutrition information per serving appears on a special panel labeled "Nutrition Facts." This panel must include the following information:

● Serving Size: Serving sizes for all foods must be consistent. For example, Brand A of macaroni and cheese must show the same amount per serving as Brand B. Consistent serving sizes allow you to easily compare the nutritional values of similar foods.

● Calories and calories from fat: Along with the number of calories per serving, the label must include the number of calories coming from fat. This number will help individuals trying to limit their fat intake to less than 30 percent calories from fat of total caloric intake (see page 6).

● Daily Values for Nutrients: The Daily Values section of the label shows how a food fits in the overall daily diet. Given as percentages, the Daily Values tell the food's nutritional content based on a 2,000-calorie-a-day diet. A 2,000-calorie diet was chosen because it falls in the midrange of the calorie spectrum for the population. Daily Values appear for those nutrients that address our biggest health concerns. These include fat, saturated fat, cholesterol, sodium, total carbohydrate, dietary fiber, vitamins A and C, calcium, and iron.

● Maximum and minimum amount of daily values: To help you see how the foods you're buying meet your needs, look near the bottom of the label. You'll see a list of six nutrients and the maximum and minimum amounts (called Daily Values) that you should strive to eat each day, depending on your caloric intake. The amounts of the first four nutrients, total fat, saturated fat, cholesterol, and sodium are maximum amounts. That is why the list says "less than" before these numbers. The amounts of total carbohydrate and dietary fiber are minimum amounts. You'll want to eat these amounts or more.

While You Cook

Besides having a written menu and the necessary foods on hand, have a meal preparation schedule in mind. Consider what should be started first, what next and so on. With each recipe in this book you'll find an estimated preparation time. Use these as guidelines in your preparation schedule.

Read the recipe before you begin. Then gather all of the ingredients and equipment you'll need. Many recipe preparations and cooking steps will overlap one another. While one part of the recipe is cooking or chilling, you can prepare another part of the recipe or even a different dish.

Many foods can be prepared completely or partially in advance. When you know you won't have time to prepare a full-fledged meal, check out the recipes with the make-ahead symbol.

Save time by chopping several onions, green peppers, or celery stalks at once when you have the knife and cutting board out on your counter. Then, freeze the items for use in recipes. You can also snip chives and parsley in quantity and then store them in the freezer.

Shredded or grated cheese is another ingredient you can prepare ahead to have on hand. When you're shredding cheese for one recipe, prepare more than you need and refrigerate the extra in a tightly sealed container.

Kitchen Organization and Equipment

In addition to planning and looking for quicker cooking techniques, it pays to take a look at your kitchen and see how you can make a more efficient place to work. Here are a few suggestions:

● Have a place for everything and keep everything in its place. You will know just where to find a specific piece of cooking equipment when you need it.

Keep equipment near the place it's used the most often. For example, store a cutting board close to the kitchen sink, where you cut up vegetables. Store pots, pans and cooking utensils near the range.

● Use as few bowls and utensils as possible to save on clean up.

● For lots of chopping, blenders and food processors are ideal for chopping and combining foods in a jiffy. But sometimes it's quicker to do it by hand.

● For small jobs, a sharp knife and cutting board may be just as fast. Keep your knives sharp. Chopping and cutting goes much more quickly with a sharp blade than with a dull one.

● A microwave oven is handy for thawing foods quickly. Also use your microwave oven for shortcuts in food preparation such as warming breads and softening or melting margarine.

● Nonstick finishes on pots and pans can save time, calories, and fat. These surfaces require less margarine or oil for cooking, and some recipes, may not need any additional fat. As a further bonus, they are easy to clean.

POULTRY PLEASERS

CHICKEN WITH MUSHROOM-PEPPERCORN SAUCE

Dress this dish up for company by substituting chanterelle or shiitake mushrooms for the white mushrooms.

4 medium chicken breast halves (1½ pounds total)
Nonstick spray coating
1 to 2 teaspoons olive oil *or* cooking oil
3 cups sliced fresh mushrooms
½ cup chopped onion
½ teaspoon dried green peppercorns, crushed
1 cup reduced-sodium chicken broth
½ cup evaporated skim milk
1 tablespoon all-purpose flour
2 tablespoons dry sherry
1 tablespoon Dijon-style mustard
2 cups hot cooked fusilli, vermicelli, *or* other pasta (optional)
Fresh sage sprigs (optional)

Remove skin from chicken. Rinse chicken; pat dry with paper towels.

Spray a cold large skillet with nonstick spray coating. Preheat skillet over medium heat. Cook chicken in hot skillet about 10 minutes, turning to brown evenly. Remove chicken from skillet.

Add 1 teaspoon oil to skillet. (Add additional 1 teaspoon oil, if necessary.) Add mushrooms, onion, and crushed peppercorns. Cook and stir for 4 to 5 minutes or till vegetables are tender. Stir in broth; return chicken pieces to skillet. Bring to boiling. Reduce heat; cover and simmer 20 minutes or till chicken is tender and no longer pink. Remove chicken.

Stir together milk and flour. Add to skillet. Cook and stir till thickened and bubbly; cook and stir for 2 minutes more. Stir in mustard and sherry; return chicken to skillet and heat through. Serve over hot cooked pasta, if desired. Garnish with fresh sage sprigs, if desired. Makes 4 servings.

Nutrition Information Per Serving: 217 calories, 5 g total fat, 1 g saturated fat, 70 mg cholesterol, 230 mg sodium, 12 g carbohydrate, 1 g fiber, 30 g protein.

APRICOT CHICKEN WITH RICE

Instead of rice, you also can serve the spicy-sweet chicken with another quick-cooking grain such as couscous or bulgur.

1¼ to 1½ **pounds meaty chicken pieces**
   Nonstick spray coating
1 **16-ounce can apricot halves** *or* **peach slices (juice pack)**
½ **cup reduced-sodium chicken broth**
1 **tablespoon reduced-sodium soy sauce**
¾ **teaspoon dried marjoram, crushed**
½ **teaspoon ground ginger**
⅛ **teaspoon bottled hot pepper sauce**
⅔ **cup long grain rice**
1 **cup chopped green pepper**
1 **tablespoon cornstarch**
1 **tablespoon water**

Remove skin from the chicken; rinse chicken and pat dry with paper towels.

Spray a cold large skillet with nonstick coating. Preheat skillet over medium heat. Cook chicken in hot skillet about 10 minutes or till chicken is lightly browned, turning to brown evenly. If necessary, drain fat.

Meanwhile, drain apricots or peaches, reserving juice. Set fruit aside. In a small bowl combine chicken broth, soy sauce, marjoram, ginger, hot pepper sauce, and reserved juice from apricots. Add broth mixture to skillet with chicken. Bring to boiling; reduce heat. Cover and simmer for 20 minutes.

Meanwhile cook rice according to package directions except omit salt and butter.

Add green pepper to skillet; cook for 4 to 5 minutes longer or till chicken is tender and no longer pink. Remove chicken to platter; keep warm.

Stir together the cornstarch, and water; stir into skillet. Cook and stir till thickened and bubbly. Cook and stir for 2 minutes more. Add apricots or peaches to skillet; heat through. Serve chicken with rice and apricot sauce. Makes 4 servings.

Nutrition Information Per Serving:
346 calories, 6 g total fat, 2 g saturated fat, 71 mg cholesterol, 264 mg sodium, 44 g carbohydrate, 2 g fiber, 27 g protein.

BUTTERMILK-CRUMB COATED CHICKEN TENDERLOIN

4 skinless, boneless, medium
  chicken breast halves
  (12 ounces total)
⅔ cup fine dry bread crumbs
¼ teaspoon paprika
⅛ teaspoon ground pepper
½ cup buttermilk
4 whole grain hamburger buns
  or Kaiser rolls, split and
  toasted
3 tablespoons nonfat
  mayonnaise dressing
4 lettuce leaves
4 slices tomato

Rinse chicken; pat dry with paper towels. Place each breast half between 2 pieces of plastic wrap. Working from the center to the edges, pound the chicken lightly with the flat side of a meat mallet to ¼-inch thickness. Remove the plastic wrap.

In a 9-inch pie plate combine bread crumbs, paprika, and pepper; mix well. Dip chicken pieces into buttermilk; then dip into crumb mixture coating evenly.

Place chicken on the unheated rack of a broiler pan. Broil 4 to 5 inches from the heat for 5 minutes. Turn chicken over and broil 5 minutes more or till chicken is tender and no longer pink and coating is golden. Spread toasted buns with the mayonnaise dressing. Serve chicken on buns with lettuce and tomato. Makes 4 servings.

Nutrition Information Per Serving:
301 calories, 6 g total fat, 2 g saturated fat, 46 mg cholesterol, 583 mg sodium, 38 g carbohydrate, 2 g fiber, 23 g protein.

The buttermilk not only helps the crumb coating stick to the chicken, it also adds a delicious, subtle tanginess to the meat.

SO LONG SKIN

Chicken meat can be a healthy part of your diet. Chicken skin cannot. So get rid of the fat by getting rid of the skin. There are two ways of doing this. First, if the chicken is cooking in a broth mixture, then remove the skin before cooking. Second, if you're baking or broiling the chicken, then remove the skin after cooking. This helps keep the meat moist and retain flavor while the fat drips away from the chicken.

SICILIAN CHICKEN

4 skinless, boneless medium
   chicken breast halves
   (12 ounces total)
   Nonstick spray coating
½ cup light ricotta cheese
1 tablespoon grated Romano *or*
   Parmesan cheese
¼ cup shredded part-skim
   mozzarella cheese
   (1 ounce)
½ of a 10-ounce package frozen
   chopped spinach, thawed
   and well drained
1 cup reduced sodium and
   reduced-fat meatless
   spaghetti sauce

Rinse chicken; pat dry with paper towels. Spray a 2-quart rectangular baking dish with nonstick coating. Place chicken pieces in dish.

Spread *2 tablespoons* of the ricotta cheese on *each* chicken breast half. Sprinkle each breast half with Romano or Parmesan cheese and mozzarella cheese. Spoon spinach evenly onto each breast half. Cover dish tightly with foil. Bake in a 350° oven about 25 minutes or till chicken is tender and no longer pink.

Meanwhile, in a small saucepan, heat spaghetti sauce. Spoon *2 tablespoons* spaghetti sauce on *each* of four plates. Place chicken on the plates; top with remaining sauce. Makes 4 servings.

Nutrition Information Per Serving:
171 calories, 6 g total fat, 2 g saturated fat, 54 mg cholesterol, 323 mg sodium, 7 g carbohydrate, 0 g fiber, 23 g protein.

To use half a package of frozen spinach, place the unwrapped spinach in a microwave-safe dish and cook on 30% power (medium-low) for 2 to 4 minutes or just till soft enough to cut in half with a sharp knife. Rewrap one half and return to freezer. Continue to cook the remaining half on 30% power for 3 to 5 minutes or more till thawed.

CHICKEN AND BULGUR PATTIES WITH CREAM GRAVY

This chicken patty was made with 85% lean ground chicken. To make it even healthier, have your butcher grind 12 ounces boneless, skinless chicken or turkey breasts to use in this and other ground poultry recipes.

¾ **cup chopped onion**
1 **large garlic clove, minced**
¼ **cup water**
3 **tablespoons bulgur**
1 **slightly beaten egg white**
½ **teaspoon dried thyme *or* marjoram, crushed**
¼ **teaspoon salt**
12 **ounces ground raw chicken *or* turkey**
1 **cup evaporated skim milk**
2 **teaspoons all-purpose flour**
1 **teaspoon instant chicken bouillon granules**
⅛ **teaspoon seasoned pepper**
½ **cup packaged cleaned spinach, stems removed and shredded**

In a medium saucepan cook onion and garlic in water about 4 minutes or till onion is tender. Stir in bulgur. Cover; let stand for 5 minutes.

Stir egg white, thyme or marjoram, and salt into bulgur mixture.

Add the chicken; mix well. Shape into four ¾-inch thick patties. Place the patties on the unheated rack of a broiler pan. Broil 3 to 4 inches from the heat for 15 to 18 minutes or till no pink remains, turning once.

Meanwhile, for gravy, in a small saucepan combine milk, flour, bouillon granules, and seasoned pepper. Cook and stir till thickened and bubbly. Cook and stir for 1 minute more. Stir in spinach; heat through. Serve patties with gravy. Makes 4 servings.

Nutrition Information Per Serving:
186 calories, 5 g total fat, 1 g saturated fat, 43 mg cholesterol, 485 mg sodium, 16 g carbohydrate, 2 g fiber, 19 g protein.

BEER-GRILLED CHICKEN

The bubbly taste of beer gives this marinade its pizazz. If you want to avoid using alcohol, choose one of the nonalcoholic beers to use, instead.

1¼ to 1½ **pounds meaty chicken**
    pieces
1 **12-ounce can beer**
    (room temperature)
3 **tablespoons reduced-sodium**
    soy sauce
2 **tablespoons brown sugar**
1 **tablespoon grated fresh**
    gingerroot
1 **teaspoon caraway seed**

Remove skin from chicken. Rinse chicken. Place chicken in a plastic bag set into a deep large bowl. For marinade, stir together beer, soy sauce, brown sugar, gingerroot, and caraway seed. Pour over chicken in bag. Seal bag and turn to coat chicken well.

Marinate in the refrigerator for 4 to 24 hours, turning bag occasionally. Drain chicken, reserving marinade.

Place chicken, bone-side up, on the grill rack, directly over *medium* coals. Grill, uncovered, for 15 minutes. Turn chicken over and grill for 10 minutes. Brush with marinade. Grill for 5 to 10 minutes more or till chicken is tender and no longer pink. Makes 4 servings.

To Grill Indirect: In a covered grill arrange medium-hot coals around a drip pan. Test for *medium* heat above the pan. Place chicken, bone-side up, on the grill rack over drip pan but not over coals. Lower the grill hood. Grill for 40 minutes, brushing occasionally with the reserved marinade. Grill for 10 to 20 minutes more (*do not* brush with marinade).

Nutrition Information Per Serving:
165 calories, 5 g total fat, 1 g saturated fat, 62 mg cholesterol, 287 mg sodium, 6 g carbohydrate, 0 g fiber, 21 g protein.

GETTING FRESH WITH GINGER

Fresh ginger, also called gingerroot, is a semitropical pungent root spice with a slightly hot flavor and nippy aroma. It's a well-known flavor in Chinese cooking, but here are a few more ideas for using this aromatic spice.

● **Ginger Vinaigrette:** Combine ½ cup salad oil, ½ cup white wine vinegar, 1 tablespoon sugar, and 1 teaspoon grated fresh gingerroot. Lightly drizzle it over a bevy of mixed greens.

● **Ginger Cream:** Stir together 1 cup reduced-fat whipped dessert topping, ½ teaspoon grated fresh gingerroot, and ¼ teaspoon vanilla. Dollop on top of fresh fruit.

● **Ginger Tea:** Add a fresh slice of gingerroot to tea with boiling water for steeping. Remove gingerroot before serving.

● **Ginger Hotcakes:** For 12 pancakes or 4 waffles, stir 1 teaspoon freshly grated gingerroot into the batter.

CHICKEN WITH CHERRY SAUCE

This slightly sweet sauce is bursting with flavor from dried tart red cherries. Look for them in cellophane packages in your grocer's produce area or on the shelf with the other dried fruits.

4 skinless, boneless medium chicken breast halves (12 ounces total)
Ground nutmeg
⅓ cup reduced-sodium chicken broth
⅓ cup unsweetened pineapple juice
2 teaspoons cornstarch
1 teaspoon brown sugar
Dash pepper
¼ cup dried tart red cherries *or* golden raisins, coarsely chopped

Rinse chicken; pat dry with paper towels. Sprinkle lightly with nutmeg. Place chicken, boned side up, on the unheated rack of a broiler pan. Broil 4 to 5 inches from the heat for 7 minutes. Turn chicken over; broil for 5 to 8 minutes more or till chicken is tender and no longer pink.

Meanwhile, for sauce, in a small saucepan combine chicken broth, pineapple juice, cornstarch, brown sugar, and pepper. Mix well. Cook and stir over medium heat till thickened and bubbly. Stir in cherries or raisins. Cook and stir for 2 minutes more. Serve chicken with cherry sauce. Makes 4 servings.

Nutrition Information Per Serving: 137 calories, 2 g total fat, 1 g saturated fat, 45 mg cholesterol, 74 mg sodium, 11 g carbohydrate, 0 g fiber, 17 g protein.

CHICKEN-MUSHROOM RAGOUT

Serve this homey,
full-flavored dish
with a crusty loaf of
bread and a fresh
green salad.

1 14½ -ounce can reduced-
   sodium chicken broth
1 tablespoon horseradish
   mustard
¼ teaspoon pepper
2 sprigs fresh thyme *or*
   ½ teaspoon dried thyme,
   crushed
4 boneless, skinless chicken
   thighs, cut into bite-size
   pieces (12 ounces total)
8 ounces fresh mushrooms,
   halved (3 cups)
1 cup sliced carrots
1 cup sliced leeks
1 cup water
2 tablespoons cornstarch

In a large saucepan or Dutch oven combine chicken broth, mustard, thyme, and pepper. Stir in chicken, mushrooms, carrots, and leeks. Bring to boiling. Reduce heat; cover and simmer 15 minutes. Remove thyme sprigs, if using.

Combine water and cornstarch. Stir into chicken mixture. Cook and stir till thickened and bubbly. Cook and stir for 2 minutes more. Serve in bowls. Makes 4 servings.

Nutrition Information Per Serving: 154 calories, 5 g total fat, 1 g saturated fat, 41 mg cholesterol, 285 mg sodium, 13 g carbohydrate, 3 g fiber, 15 g protein.

CHICKEN IN A BUN

4 skinless, boneless medium
   chicken breast halves
   (12 ounces total)
1 tablespoon reduced-sodium
   soy sauce
   Nonstick spray coating
2 tablespoons nonfat Italian
   salad dressing
4 whole-grain hamburger
   buns, toasted
4 lettuce leaves
4 tomato slices
4 thin red onion slices

Rinse chicken; pat dry with paper towels. Brush with soy sauce.

Spray a cold large skillet with nonstick spray coating. Preheat skillet over medium heat. Add chicken to skillet; cook for 8 to 10 minutes or till chicken is tender and no longer pink, turning once.

Drizzle chicken with salad dressing. Serve chicken on toasted buns with lettuce, tomato, and onion. Makes 4 servings.

Nutrition Information Per Serving:
269 calories, 5 g total fat, 1 g saturated fat, 45 mg cholesterol, 533 mg sodium, 33 g carbohydrate, 4 g fiber, 22 g protein.

Skip the fast food restaurants and make your own chicken sandwich at home. This tasty version is low in fat and calories and only takes 15 minutes to make.

SANDWICH SAVVY

Sandwiches are not only quick and easy to prepare, but they can be a healthy part of anyone's diet. So start stacking, but put these healthy tips to work before you begin.

● Use whole grain bread or rolls for increased fiber. Choose bread or rolls that list whole wheat flour (or another whole grain flour) as the first ingredient.

● Take control of the amount of fat and sodium in your sandwich meat by cooking and thinly slicing your own instead of using processed luncheon meats. A good choice: one 2½- to 3-pound skinless turkey breast half with bone roasted in a 325° oven for 2½ to 3 hours or till a meat thermometer registers 165°.

● Get rid of fat-laden mayonnaise, margarine, and butter and spread full-flavored mustard, nonfat mayonnaise dressing, fat-free salad dressing, or apple butter on your bread.

● Check out the dairy case to find a growing selection of reduced-fat and fat-free cheeses. Use these instead of their higher-fat cousins.

● Don't forget the fresh veggies! Leaf lettuce, colorful sweet peppers, red onions, cucumbers, tomatoes, and shredded carrots all add color, texture, flavor, fiber, and vitamins.

CHICKEN MARGARITA

4 skinless, boneless medium
    chicken breast halves
    (12 ounces total)
½ teaspoon ground coriander
⅛ teaspoon salt
    Dash pepper
    Nonstick spray coating
1 tablespoon lime juice
2 teaspoons cornstarch
½ teaspoon sugar
½ cup reduced-sodium chicken
    broth
¼ cup orange juice
1 to 2 tablespoons snipped
    cilantro
1 tablespoon tequila
    Lime slices
    (optional)
    Fresh cilantro leaves
    (optional)

Rinse chicken; pat dry with paper towels. Combine coriander, salt, and pepper. Rub spice mixture onto chicken on both sides. Spray a cold large skillet with nonstick coating. Preheat skillet over medium heat. Cook chicken in hot skillet for 8 to 10 minutes or till tender and no longer pink, turning once. Remove chicken from skillet; keep chicken warm.

For sauce, combine lime juice, cornstarch, and sugar; set aside. Carefully add chicken broth and orange juice to hot skillet. Stir in lime juice mixture. Cook and stir till thickened and bubbly. Cook for 1 minute more. Stir in cilantro and tequila. Spoon sauce over chicken. Garnish with lime slices and cilantro leaves, if desired. Makes 4 servings.

Nutrition Information Per Serving:
119 calories, 3 g total fat, 1 g saturated fat, 45 mg cholesterol, 377 mg sodium, 4 g carbohydrate, 0 g fiber, 16 g protein.

If the thought of a frosty margarita makes your mouth water, then this tasty chicken dish will, too. That's because it's flavored with margarita fixin's such as lime juice and tequila.

CHICKEN WITH TOASTED SESAME SEED GLAZE

Serve these mustard-and sesame-seasoned chicken breasts with either quick-to-fix couscous or quick-cooking rice.

4 skinless, boneless, medium chicken breast halves (12 ounces total)

2 teaspoons olive oil *or* cooking oil

2 teaspoons sesame seed

⅔ cup reduced-sodium chicken broth

2 teaspoons Dijon-style *or* country-style mustard

1 teaspoon cornstarch

Rinse chicken; pat dry with paper towels. In a large skillet heat oil; add sesame seed. Toast for 1 minute over medium heat. Add chicken. Cook for 8 to 10 minutes or till chicken is tender and no longer pink, turning the pieces occasionally to brown evenly and to coat with sesame seed.

Remove chicken to a serving platter; keep warm. Stir together chicken broth, mustard, and cornstarch. Carefully add broth mixture to skillet; cook and stir till thickened and bubbly. Cook and stir for 2 minutes more. Pour over chicken. Makes 4 servings.

Nutrition Information Per Serving: 126 calories, 6 g total fat, 1 g saturated fat, 45 mg cholesterol, 171 mg sodium, 1 g carbohydrate, 0 g fiber, 17 g protein.

MICROWAVE QUICK-THAW

Ooops! Forget to defrost the chicken or turkey for tonight's dinner? Don't worry, as long as you have a microwave oven. Use the chart below as a guide to defrosting your frozen fowl. Before you begin, unwrap the frozen poultry and place it in a microwave-safe dish. Cover with a lid or plastic wrap and defrost on 30% power (medium-low) for the time listed below. Stir, turn, or separate the food halfway through cooking. Let it stand for a few minutes to complete thawing.

		AMOUNT	MINUTES
Chicken	cut-up	2½ to 3 lb.	15 to 17
	breasts	1½ lb.	12 to 14
	drumsticks	6 drumsticks	8 to 10
	ground	1 lb.	10 to 12
Turkey	breast half	3 to 4 lb.	20 to 25
	tenderloin	1 lb.	8 to 10
	ground	1 lb.	10 to 12

CHICKEN MEATBALLS WITH YOGURT-DILL SAUCE

6 ounces egg noodles
  Nonstick spray coating
1 slightly beaten egg white
1 8-ounce carton plain lowfat
  yogurt
¼ cup fine dry bread crumbs
2 tablespoons snipped fresh dill
  or 1½ teaspoons dried
  dillweed
1 teaspoon white wine
  Worcestershire sauce
⅛ teaspoon pepper
12 ounces ground raw chicken
  or turkey
3 tablespoons all-purpose flour
1 cup reduced-sodium
  chicken broth

Cook noodles according to package directions *except* omit salt and butter; keep warm.

Meanwhile, spray a shallow baking pan with nonstick spray coating; set aside. In a medium bowl combine beaten egg white, *2 tablespoons* of the yogurt, bread crumbs, *half* of the dill, Worcestershire sauce, and pepper. Add ground chicken; mix well. To form meatballs, drop the chicken mixture by rounded teaspoons into prepared baking pan. Bake in a 400° oven about 20 minutes or till no pink remains.

While meatballs bake, in a medium saucepan stir together the remaining yogurt and flour; add broth and remaining dill. Cook and stir till thickened and bubbly. Cook and stir for 1 minute more. Stir in meatballs; heat through. Serve over hot noodles. Serves 4.

Nutrition Information Per Serving: 330 calories, 8 g total fat, 2 g saturated fat, 81 mg cholesterol, 259 mg sodium, 41 g carbohydrate, 0 g fiber, 23 g protein.

For a picture-perfect plate, serve these saucy meatballs over hot cooked spinach egg noodles.

CHICKEN STEW WITH GREMOLATA

Gremolata is a flavor-packed blend of fresh parsley, garlic, and lemon peel that you sprinkle on each serving of this hearty chicken stew.

1¼ to 1½ pounds meaty chicken pieces
   Nonstick spray coating
1 pound new potatoes
2 cups tiny whole carrots
1 cup frozen small whole onions
2 stalks celery, cut into 1-inch pieces
1 cup reduced-sodium chicken broth
½ cup dry white wine *or* reduced-sodium chicken broth
½ teaspoon dried oregano, crushed
¼ teaspoon dried thyme, crushed
1 medium zucchini, halved lengthwise and cut into ½-inch pieces
½ cup evaporated skim milk
3 tablespoons all-purpose flour
   Gremolata

Remove skin from chicken. Rinse chicken; pat dry with paper towels. Spray a cold very large saucepan or 4½-quart Dutch oven with nonstick spray coating. Preheat pan over medium heat. Cook chicken in hot pan about 10 minutes or till lightly browned, turning to brown evenly. If necessary, drain fat.

Cut any large potatoes in half. Add potatoes, carrots, onions, celery, broth, wine, oregano, and thyme. Bring to boiling. Reduce heat; cover and simmer for 20 minutes. Add zucchini; cook for 5 minutes more or till chicken and vegetables are tender. Remove chicken pieces; keep warm.

Stir together milk and flour. Stir into hot mixture. Cook and stir till thickened and bubbly. Cook and stir for 1 minute more. Return chicken to mixture. Heat through. Serve in large shallow soup bowls and sprinkle each serving with Gremolata. Makes 4 servings.

Gremolata: In a small bowl combine 3 tablespoons snipped *parsley;* 1 large clove *garlic*, minced; and 1 teaspoon finely shredded *lemon peel*. Toss to mix.

Nutrition Information Per Serving: 348 calories, 5 g total fat, 1 g saturated fat, 59 mg cholesterol, 248 mg sodium, 45 g carbohydrate, 3 g fiber, 27 g protein.

SPICY CHICKEN AND MELON KABOBS

Keep these fruity kabobs in mind the next time you have a backyard barbecue. Instead of broiling them, cook the kabobs directly over hot coals for 8 to 10 minutes or till chicken is tender and no longer pink.

1 tablespoon olive oil *or* cooking oil
2 cloves garlic, minced
½ teaspoon dried rosemary, crushed
¼ teaspoon ground cumin
⅛ teaspoon salt
⅛ teaspoon ground coriander
⅛ teaspoon ground black pepper
   Dash ground red pepper
2 tablespoons balsamic vinegar *or* red wine vinegar
4 skinless, boneless medium chicken breast halves (12 ounces total)
½ medium cantaloupe, peeled and cut into 1½-inch pieces
16 green onions, cut into 2-inch pieces
2 tablespoons peach *or* apricot preserves

In a small saucepan heat oil; add garlic, rosemary, cumin, salt, coriander, and pepper. Heat and stir for 1 minute. Remove from heat; cool slightly. Stir in vinegar. Set aside.

Rinse chicken; pat dry with paper towels. Cut each breast half into 1-inch pieces. On four 12- to 15-inch skewers, alternately thread chicken with cantaloupe and green onion. Brush all surfaces with vinegar mixture. Place skewers on the unheated rack of a broiler pan.

Broil kabobs 4 to 5 inches from heat for 5 minutes. Stir preserves into remaining vinegar mixture. Brush on kabobs; turn kabobs and brush again. Broil 3 to 5 minutes more or till chicken is tender and no longer pink. Makes 4 servings.

Nutrition Information Per Serving: 213 calories, 6 g total fat, 1 g saturated fat, 45 mg cholesterol, 142 mg sodium, 23 g carbohydrate, 2 g fiber, 18 g protein.

IS IT FRESH OR FROZEN?

Don't be surprised to find a package of chicken in your supermarket's fresh meat case that feels "frozen." According to the USDA it's OK if poultry companies chill their fresh products to around 26 degrees F. after processing. This low temperature slows bacterial growth and increases the shelf life of the poultry. Even though the package may feel frozen, the inside of the meat is not frozen. So treat the meat just as you would any other fresh meat by taking it directly home from the store and refrigerating it or freezing it immediately. Use refrigerated poultry within one or two days and frozen poultry within nine to twelve months.

SAGE AND LEEK BRAISED CHICKEN

45

1¼ to 1½ pounds meaty chicken
    pieces
    Nonstick spray coating
1 cup reduced-sodium chicken
    broth
2 medium leeks, thinly sliced
    or ⅔ cup thinly sliced green
    onion
2 tablespoons snipped fresh
    sage *or* 1½ teaspoons dried
    leaf sage, crushed
¼ teaspoon nutmeg
¼ teaspoon pepper
6 ounces medium noodles
1 tablespoon corn syrup *or*
    granulated sugar
1 tablespoon lemon juice *or*
    white wine vinegar
1 tablespoon water
2 teaspoons cornstarch

Remove skin from chicken. Rinse chicken; pat dry with paper towels. Spray a cold large skillet with nonstick coating. Preheat over medium heat. Cook chicken in hot skillet about 10 minutes or till lightly browned, turning to brown evenly. If necessary, drain fat.

Stir in chicken broth, sliced leeks or green onion, sage, nutmeg, and pepper. Bring to boiling; reduce heat. Cover and simmer about 25 minutes or till chicken is tender and no longer pink.

Meanwhile, cook the noodles according to package directions except omit salt. Drain and keep warm.

Remove chicken from skillet; keep warm. For sauce, stir together the corn syrup, lemon juice, water, and cornstarch. Stir into skillet. Cook and stir till thickened and bubbly. Cook and stir for 2 minutes more. Spoon sauce over chicken. Serve with hot cooked noodles. Makes 4 servings.

Nutrition Information Per Serving:
305 calories, 6 g total fat, 2 g saturated fat, 94 mg cholesterol, 166 mg sodium, 36 g carbohydrate, 1 g fiber, 25 g protein.

Be sure to wash the leeks thoroughly to remove all the dirt and grit that tends to get imbedded in them.

CRISPY CHICKEN STICKS

**2 skinless, boneless medium
chicken breasts
(12 ounces total)**
⅓ cup cornflake crumbs
¼ cup yellow cornmeal
**1 tablespoon grated Parmesan
cheese**
**⅛ teaspoon ground red pepper
(optional)**
**⅓ cup all-purpose flour
Nonstick spray coating**
½ cup plain nonfat yogurt
**1 tablespoon prepared
mustard *or* Dijon-style
mustard
Celery sticks *and/or* carrot
slices (optional)
Celery leaves (optional)**

Rinse chicken; pat dry with paper towels. Cut chicken into pieces about 1x3½-inches.

In a shallow bowl combine cornflake crumbs, cornmeal, Parmesan cheese, and, if desired, red pepper. Dip each chicken piece in flour, then in a little water. Roll in cornmeal mixture to coat.

Spray a baking sheet with non-stick coating. Place chicken on the baking sheet. Bake in a 375° oven for 20 to 25 minutes or till tender and no longer pink.

Meanwhile, for dipping sauce, stir together yogurt and mustard. Serve chicken with dipping sauce. If desired, serve with celery sticks and carrot slices and garnish with celery leaves. Makes 4 servings.

Nutrition Information Per Serving:
203 calories, 4 g total fat, 1 g saturated fat, 46 mg cholesterol, 169 mg sodium, 20 g carbohydrate, 1 g fiber, 21 g protein.

For easy kitchen cleanup, line the baking sheet with foil before spraying it with nonstick coating.

GREEK CHICKEN PITA

Good-bye plain hamburgers and hello spice-exploding chicken burgers. They're tucked inside pita halves and are topped with a creamy cucumber and mint relish.

2 tablespoons skim milk

3 tablespoons fine dry bread crumbs

½ teaspoon dried oregano, crushed

½ teaspoon ground cumin

½ teaspoon ground coriander

¼ teaspoon garlic salt

¼ teaspoon pepper

12 ounces ground raw chicken *or* turkey

½ cup plain nonfat yogurt

½ small cucumber, seeded and chopped (⅓ cup)

1 green onion, thinly sliced

2 teaspoons snipped fresh mint *or* ½ teaspoon dried mint, crushed

⅛ teaspoon sugar

2 pita bread rounds, halved crosswise

1 cup shredded fresh spinach *or* lettuce

In a medium mixing bowl combine milk, bread crumbs, oregano, cumin, coriander, garlic salt, and pepper. Add ground chicken or turkey; mix well. Form into 4 oval patties about ½-inch thick.

Place patties on the unheated rack of a broiler pan. Broil 4 to 5 inches from the heat for 5 minutes. Turn over and broil 5 to 10 minutes more or till chicken is no longer pink.

Meanwhile, in a small bowl stir together the yogurt, chopped cucumber, onion, mint, and sugar. Mix well.

Split open each pita half forming a pocket. Place some of the spinach or lettuce and a chicken patty in the pocket; top with yogurt mixture and remaining spinach. Makes 4 servings.

Nutrition Information Per Serving: 177 calories, 5 g total fat, 1 g saturated fat, 41 mg cholesterol, 326 mg sodium, 16 g carbohydrate, 1 g fiber, 17 g protein.

POULTRY POINTERS

Buying fresh poultry is as easy as peering into the meat case at your grocery store. To ensure that you're getting a fresh bird, do a quick quality check. For all types of poultry, be sure the package is securely sealed and there is no unpleasant or off odor. For pieces with skin, avoid those with pinfeathers and bruises.

CHICKEN AND ONIONS WITH ORANGE SAUCE

4 skinless, boneless medium
   chicken breast halves
   (12 ounces total)
  Nonstick spray coating
  Pepper
  Dash salt
2 teaspoons olive oil *or* cooking
   oil
2 medium onions, thinly sliced
   and separated into rings
1 8-ounce carton plain nonfat
   yogurt
¼ cup water
2 tablespoons all-purpose flour
¼ cup reduced-calorie orange
   marmalade
2 cups hot cooked rice *or* pasta
  Orange slices *or* orange peel
   (optional)

Rinse chicken; pat dry with paper towels. Spray a cold large skillet with nonstick spray coating. Preheat skillet over medium heat. Sprinkle chicken with pepper and salt. Cook chicken in hot skillet for 8 to 10 minutes or till tender and no longer pink, turning once. Remove chicken; keep warm.

For sauce, add oil and onions to skillet. Cook and stir onions over medium heat about 5 minutes or till tender. In a small bowl, combine yogurt, water, and flour; mix well. Stir into onions. Cook and stir till thickened and bubbly. Cook and stir for 1 minute more. Stir in marmalade. Serve chicken with sauce over cooked rice or pasta. Garnish with orange slices or peel, if desired. Makes 4 servings.

Nutrition Information Per Serving:
330 calories, 6 g total fat, 1 g saturated fat, 45 mg cholesterol, 100 mg sodium, 48 g carbohydrate, 3 g fiber, 21 g protein.

Orange marmalade stars in this sauce to give a winning flavor and beautiful color to the chicken.

ANGEL HAIR PASTA WITH CHICKEN AND SHRIMP

First things first: heat the water for the pasta before you begin the rest of the recipe. To shave off a few minutes, use fresh, refrigerated pasta.

4 ounces fresh *or* frozen peeled medium shrimp
½ cup reduced-sodium chicken broth
2 tablespoons reduced-sodium soy sauce
2 teaspoons cornstarch
½ teaspoon ground ginger
8 ounces skinless, boneless chicken breast halves *or* turkey breast tenderloin steak
6 ounces angel hair pasta
Nonstick spray coating
1 to 2 teaspoons cooking oil (optional)
½ cup green onions, cut into ½-inch pieces
2 garlic cloves, minced
1 yellow summer squash, sliced (1¼ cups)
1 small red *or* green sweet pepper, cut into thin strips

Thaw shrimp, if frozen. In a small mixing bowl combine the chicken broth, soy sauce, cornstarch, and ginger; set aside.

Rinse chicken; pat dry with paper towels. Cut chicken into ¾-inch pieces; set aside. Cook pasta according to package directions *except* omit salt and oil. Drain and keep warm.

Meanwhile, spray a cold large skillet with nonstick spray coating. (Add oil if necessary, during cooking.) Preheat skillet over medium heat. Add green onion and garlic; stir-fry for 1 minute. Remove from skillet. Add squash to skillet; stir-fry for 1½ minutes. Add red or green pepper; stir-fry for 1½ minutes more or till vegetables are crisp-tender. Remove vegetables from skillet.

Add chicken and shrimp to skillet; stir-fry for 3 to 4 minutes or till chicken is no longer pink and shrimp turns opaque. Push chicken and shrimp from the center of the skillet. Stir broth mixture; add to center of the skillet. Cook and stir till thickened and bubbly. Return all of the cooked vegetables to skillet; stir all ingredients together to coat with sauce. Cook and stir about 1 minute more or till heated through. Serve hot chicken mixture over pasta. Makes 4 servings.

Nutrition Information Per Serving:
268 calories, 5 g total fat, 1 g saturated fat, 110 mg cholesterol, 413 mg sodium, 33 g carbohydrate, 2 g fiber, 23 g protein.

CHICKEN CURRY

When testing this spicy dish, we discovered low-fat yogurt makes a smoother sauce than nonfat yogurt, and keeps the fat total to 6 grams per serving.

⅔ **cup long grain rice**
8 **ounces skinless, boneless chicken breast halves**
½ **cup chopped onion**
2 **garlic cloves, minced**
1 **tablespoon curry powder**
1 **tablespoon margarine**
¼ **cup apricot preserves**
1 **medium apple, cut into bite-size pieces**
¼ **cup raisins**
⅓ **cup water**
¼ **teaspoon salt**
1½ **cups plain low-fat yogurt**
2 **tablespoons cornstarch**

Cook rice according to package directions omitting salt and butter.

Rinse chicken; pat dry with paper towels. Thinly slice chicken across the grain into bite-size strips or cut into small cubes. Set chicken aside.

In a large nonstick skillet cook onion, garlic, and curry powder in margarine for 1 minute. Push onion mixture to side of skillet.

Cook chicken in hot skillet over medium heat for 3 to 5 minutes or till chicken is lightly browned and no longer pink. Stir chicken and onion mixture together.

Cut any large pieces of the apricot preserves in half. Stir preserves, apple, raisins, water, and salt into chicken mixture.

Stir together yogurt and cornstarch. Stir into chicken mixture. Cook and stir till thickened and bubbly. Cook and stir for 2 minutes more. Serve over hot cooked rice. Makes 4 servings.

Nutrition Information Per Serving:
381 calories, 6 g total fat, 2 g saturated fat, 35 mg cholesterol, 261 mg sodium, 63 g carbohydrate, 2 g fiber, 19 g protein.

POTATO-TOPPED CHICKEN

 45

Nonstick spray coating
4 **skinless, boneless medium
    chicken breast halves
    (12 ounces total)**
2 **frozen shredded hash brown
    potato patties, thawed**
1 **small onion, finely chopped
    (⅓ cup)**
1 **slightly beaten egg white**
2 **teaspoons cooking oil**
⅛ **teaspoon pepper**
8 **small fresh basil leaves**
2 **tablespoons grated Parmesan
    cheese**

Spray a baking sheet with non-stick spray coating. Set aside.

Rinse chicken; pat dry with paper towels; set aside.

In a medium bowl toss together potatoes and onion, breaking up potato patties. Stir in egg white, oil, and pepper; set aside.

Place chicken on a baking sheet. Place 2 fresh basil leaves on each chicken piece. With hands, top each chicken piece with potato mixture. Sprinkle each piece with Parmesan cheese.

Bake in a 450° oven about 15 minutes or till chicken is tender and no longer pink and potato mixture is brown. Serves 4.

Nutrition Information Per Serving:
158 calories, 6 g total fat, 2 g saturated fat, 47 mg cholesterol, 118 mg sodium, 6 g carbohydrate, 1 g fiber, 19 g protein.

Don't worry if your hash browns are frozen solid. You can thaw them quickly in your microwave oven by placing them in a microwave-safe bowl and cooking them on 100% power (high) for 2 minutes, stirring once.

MAKE-AHEAD PASTA AND RICE

Take advantage of a few spare minutes now to cook pasta or rice to use later. Simply cook the desired amount of pasta or rice according to package directions, except omit margarine or butter. Rinse pasta or rice and drain well. Line 6-ounce custard cups with clear plastic wrap. Spoon ½ cup cooked pasta or rice into lined custard cups. Seal, label, and freeze in custard cups till firm. Remove from custard cups and wrap each portion in clear plastic wrap. Place wrapped portions in a large freezer bag. Seal, label, and freeze up to 6 months. To reheat frozen pasta, unwrap desired amount. Using a large spoon, carefully lower pasta into boiling water in a saucepan. Return to boiling and cook for 1 minute. Drain. To reheat frozen rice, unwrap desired amount of frozen rice and place in a saucepan. Add 1 tablespoon of water for each ½ cup frozen rice. Cover and heat about 5 minutes or till hot, stirring occasionally. To reheat pasta or rice in a microwave oven, unwrap frozen pasta or rice and return to custard cups. Cover with waxed paper and micro-cook on 100% power (high) till hot. Allow 1½ to 2 minutes for one ½-cup portion or 2 to 2½ minutes for 2 portions.

CHICKEN MOLE WITH PUMPKIN SEEDS

4 skinless, boneless medium
    chicken breast halves *or*
    large skinless, boneless
    chicken thighs
    (12 ounces total)
    Nonstick spray coating
1 teaspoon olive oil *or*
    cooking oil
¼ cup finely chopped onion
2 cloves garlic, minced
1½ teaspoons chili powder
½ teaspoon ground cumin
1 8-ounce can reduced-sodium
    tomato sauce
2 tablespoons raisins
2 tablespoons snipped cilantro
    or ½ teaspoon ground
    coriander
2 tablespoons toasted hulled
    pumpkin seeds, sunflower
    seeds, *or* sliced almonds
1 teaspoon unsweetened cocoa
    powder
½ teaspoon instant chicken
    bouillon granules
2 cups hot cooked rice
    Carrot strips (optional)
    Cilantro sprigs (optional)

Rinse chicken; pat dry with paper towels. Spray a 2-quart rectangular baking dish with nonstick spray coating. Place chicken in dish. Bake, uncovered, in a 400° oven for 15 minutes.

Meanwhile, for the sauce, in a medium saucepan heat the oil. Cook the onion and garlic in the hot oil for 2 minutes. Stir in chili powder and cumin; cook for 1 minute. Stir in tomato sauce, raisins, cilantro, *1 tablespoon* of the pumpkin seeds, cocoa powder, and bouillon granules. Bring to boiling. Reduce heat; cover and simmer for 3 minutes.

Transfer sauce to a blender container or food processor bowl. Cover and blend or process till sauce is nearly smooth.

Spoon about *2 tablespoons* of the mole sauce over each piece of chicken. Bake for 5 to 10 minutes more or till chicken is tender and no longer pink.

Serve chicken over hot cooked rice. Sprinkle chicken with remaining pumpkin seeds. Garnish with carrot strips and cilantro sprigs, if desired. Pass remaining sauce. Makes 4 servings.

Nutrition Information Per Serving:
267 calories, 6 g total fat, 1 g saturated fat, 45 mg cholesterol, 180 mg sodium, 31 g carbohydrate, 2 g fiber, 21 g protein.

A Mexican mole (MOH-lay) sauce contains a piquant combination of seasonings and chocolate or cocoa powder. Serve this streamlined version with 2 cups of hot cooked rice.

SPICED CHICKEN BURGERS WITH MUSTARD GLAZE

This clever burger can double as a breakfast meat. Simply substitute 12 ounces of ground turkey sausage for the ground raw chicken or turkey.

2 tablespoons fine dry bread crumbs
¼ teaspoon dried thyme, crushed
¼ teaspoon ground nutmeg
⅛ teaspoon ground red pepper
⅛ teaspoon ground allspice
Dash ground cloves
1 slightly beaten egg white
12 ounces ground raw chicken *or* turkey
Nonstick spray coating
3 tablespoons reduced-calorie pancake and waffle syrup
1 tablespoon Dijon-style mustard

In a large bowl stir together bread crumbs, thyme, nutmeg, red pepper, allspice, and cloves. Stir in egg white and ground chicken or turkey; mix well. Shape into 4 patties, about ½- to ¾-inch thick.

Spray a large skillet with non-stick spray coating. Preheat over medium heat. Cook chicken patties in the skillet for 10 to 15 minutes, or till patties are brown and no pink remains, turning once. For glaze, stir together syrup and mustard; add to skillet all at once. Turn patties once to coat with glaze. Makes 4 servings.

Nutrition Information Per Serving: 132 calories, 5 g total fat, 1 g saturated fat, 41 mg cholesterol, 201 mg sodium, 7 g carbohydrate, 0 g fiber, 14 g protein.

SESAME CHICKEN WITH LEMON SAUCE

4 skinless, boneless medium
   chicken breast halves
   (12 ounces total)
1 teaspoon toasted sesame oil
⅛ teaspoon pepper
⅔ cup reduced-sodium chicken
   broth
4 green onions, thinly sliced
   (¼ cup)
1 tablespoon sesame seed,
   toasted
½ teaspoon finely shredded
   lemon peel
1 tablespoon lemon juice
2 teaspoons cornstarch

Rinse chicken; pat dry with paper towels. Rub sesame oil on both sides of chicken pieces; sprinkle with pepper. Place chicken on the unheated rack of a broiler pan. Broil 4 to 5 inches from the heat for 5 minutes. Turn chicken; broil for 5 to 7 minutes more or till tender and no longer pink.

Meanwhile, in a medium saucepan combine chicken broth, green onion, sesame seed, lemon peel, lemon juice, and cornstarch. Cook and stir till thickened and bubbly. Cook and stir for 2 minutes more. Pour sauce over chicken. Makes 4 servings.

Nutrition Information Per Serving:
121 calories, 5 g total fat, 1 g saturated fat, 45 mg cholesterol, 108 mg sodium, 2 g carbohydrate, 0 g fiber, 17 g protein.

The rich sesame flavor comes from a combination of the toasted sesame seed and toasted sesame oil. Look for toasted sesame oil at your supermarket, specialty food store or Oriental grocer.

HOW ABOUT A DATE?

You bet! Especially when the date is the one stamped on poultry products, dairy foods, meats, and some packaged products. These "sell-by," "use-by," or other dates are your guarantee that these products are fresh up until the date that is displayed on the package.

Select packages dated furthest into the future and be sure you have ample time to use them. If you aren't able to use the product before the date expires, freeze the food, if possible. Avoid any products that are beyond the "use-by" date and notify the store manager or department manager so they can remove the expired items from the shelves.

CHICKEN WITH CITRUS-LEEK SAUCE

This easy orange and leek sauce also goes great with lean roasted pork or grilled fish.

4 **skinless, boneless medium chicken breast halves (12 ounces total)**
1 **medium leek, thinly sliced (about ½ cup)**
2 **teaspoons cooking oil**
½ **cup orange-grapefruit juice**
2 **tablespoons dry vermouth *or* dry white wine**
2 **tablespoons reduced-calorie orange marmalade**
2 **cups hot cooked couscous *or* rice (optional)**

Rinse the chicken; pat dry with paper towels.

In a large skillet, cook leeks in hot oil over medium heat for 2 minutes; remove from skillet. Add chicken; cook for 8 to 10 minutes or till tender and no longer pink, turning once. Remove chicken; keep warm.

Add orange-grapefruit juice, vermouth, and marmalade to the skillet. Bring to boiling. Reduce heat. Boil gently about 3 minutes or till liquid is reduced by half. Return chicken and leeks to skillet, turning chicken to coat with glaze. Heat through. Serve with hot cooked couscous or rice, if desired. Makes 4 servings.

Nutrition Information Per Serving: 164 calories, 5 g total fat, 1 g saturated fat, 45 mg cholesterol, 43 mg sodium, 12 g carbohydrate, 1 g fiber, 16 g protein.

CHICKEN CHILI BLANCO

This white chicken chili is chock full of beans, vegetables, and flavor. Serve it with a healthy salad of mixed greens.

6 ounces skinless, boneless chicken breasts *or* thighs
Nonstick spray coating
1 large onion, finely chopped (1 cup)
2 cloves garlic, minced
1 cup reduced-sodium chicken broth
2 cups sliced fresh mushrooms
1 15½-ounce can reduced-sodium kidney beans, rinsed and drained
1 8½-ounce can cream-style corn
½ cup chopped red *or* green sweet pepper
½ cup dry white wine
1 4-ounce can diced green chilies, drained
1 teaspoon ground cumin
1 teaspoon dried oregano, crushed
Dash salt
¼ cup snipped fresh parsley

Rinse the chicken; pat dry with paper towels. Cut the chicken into 1-inch pieces.

Spray a large saucepan with nonstick spray coating. Preheat saucepan over medium heat. Add chicken, onion, and garlic. Cook about 2 minutes or till chicken is no longer pink. Stir in chicken broth, mushrooms, kidney beans, corn, chopped pepper, wine, chilies, cumin, oregano, and salt. Bring to boiling. Reduce heat; cover and simmer for 10 minutes. Stir in parsley. Makes 4 servings.

Nutrition Information Per Serving:
240 calories, 3 g total fat, 0 g saturated fat, 22 mg cholesterol, 628 mg sodium, 39 g carbohydrate, 7 g fiber, 18 g protein.

LINGUINE WITH CHICKEN AND CLAM SAUCE

8 ounces linguine *or* fettuccine
  Nonstick spray coating
½ pound ground raw chicken
    or turkey
1 medium onion, chopped
    (½ cup)
2 cloves garlic, minced
½ teaspoon dried basil, crushed
⅛ teaspoon salt
⅛ teaspoon pepper
¼ cup all-purpose flour
1¼ cups reduced-sodium chicken
    broth
¾ cup evaporated skim milk
¼ cup snipped parsley
¼ cup dry white wine
1 10-ounce can whole baby
    clams, drained

Cook pasta according to package directions *except* omit salt and oil. Keep warm.

Meanwhile, spray a large saucepan with nonstick spray coating. Cook chicken or turkey, onion, garlic, basil, salt, and pepper till chicken is no longer pink and onion is tender. Stir in flour. Add chicken broth and milk. Cook and stir till thickened and bubbly. Cook and stir for 1 minute more. Stir in clams, parsley, and wine; heat through. Serve sauce over hot pasta. Makes 4 servings.

Nutrition Information Per Serving: 407 calories, 5 g total fat, 1 g saturated fat, 43 mg cholesterol, 301 mg sodium, 60 g carbohydrate, 1 g fiber, 26 g protein.

You can make the sauce taste a little richer by omitting the wine and increasing the evaporated skim milk to 1 cup.

LESS MESS

To help get you in and out of the kitchen in record time, follow these simple cleanup tips.

● Crusty broiler pans: Coat surface of dirty pan with dishwashing liquid. Cover with a damp paper towel and let stand till crust softens.

● Burned pots and pans: Do not run cold water into your hot pans because this can warp them. Instead, let the pan cool and fill with water, adding a little baking soda. Boil gently till the food loosens. For aluminum pots and pans, do not use baking soda. Boil water in pans till the food loosens. Then wash the pots and pans with hot soapy water.

BROILED CHICKEN WITH FRESH PLUM SAUCE

4 **skinless, boneless medium chicken breast halves (12 ounces total)**

3 **medium purple *or* blue plums, pitted and sliced (1½ cups)**

½ **cup grape juice**

1 **teaspoon finely snipped fresh rosemary *or* ¼ teaspoon dried rosemary, crushed**

½ **teaspoon sugar**

1 **tablespoon water**

2 **teaspoons cornstarch**

2 **tablespoons snipped parsley (optional)**

2 **cups hot cooked rice (optional)**

   Fresh rosemary sprigs (optional)

Rinse chicken; pat dry with paper towels. Place chicken on the unheated rack of a broiler pan. Broil 4 to 5 inches from heat for 5 minutes. Turn chicken; broil for 7 to 10 minutes more or till chicken is tender and no longer pink.

Meanwhile, for sauce, in a medium saucepan combine sliced plums, grape juice, rosemary, and sugar. Bring to boiling; reduce heat. Cover and simmer for 3 minutes. Stir together the water and cornstarch; stir into the plum mixture. Cook and stir till thickened and bubbly. Cook and stir for 2 minutes more.

If desired, stir parsley into rice. Serve chicken with rice and top with sauce. Garnish with additional fresh rosemary, if desired. Makes 4 servings.

Nutrition Information Per Serving: 134 calories, 2 g total fat, 1 g saturated fat, 45 mg cholesterol, 42 mg sodium, 11 g carbohydrate, 0 g fiber, 16 g protein.

Serve this fruity chicken to family or friends when plums are at their best. Look for them at your supermarket from June through September.

CRUNCHY FETA-TOPPED CHICKEN

Turn this crunchy chicken topping into a mushroom stuffing to serve as an appetizer. Simply spoon the crumb mixture into the mushroom caps and broil for 5 to 10 minutes.

6 skinless, boneless medium chicken breast halves (1¼ pounds total)
⅔ cup soft bread crumbs
⅓ cup finely crumbled feta cheese (about 1½ ounces)
¼ cup finely chopped fresh mushrooms
¼ cup Grape Nuts cereal
2 green onions, finely chopped (2 tablespoons)
1 teaspoon olive oil *or* cooking oil
¼ teaspoon pepper

Rinse chicken; pat dry with paper towels. Place chicken, boned side down, on the unheated rack of a broiler pan. Broil 4 to 5 inches from the heat for 10 minutes.

Meanwhile, in a small mixing bowl combine bread crumbs, cheese, mushrooms, cereal, green onion, oil, and pepper. Toss to mix well; set aside.

Turn chicken boned side up. Spoon crumb mixture in an even layer onto each chicken breast half. Broil for 2 to 5 minutes more or till crumbs are brown and chicken is tender and no longer pink. Makes 6 servings.

Nutrition Information Per Serving:
158 calories, 5 g total fat, 2 g saturated fat, 56 mg cholesterol, 183 mg sodium, 7 g carbohydrate, 0 g fiber, 20 g protein.

FABULOUS
FISH

TUNA WITH TOMATO-ARUGULA SALSA

1 pound fresh *or* frozen tuna *or* swordfish steaks
½ pound plum tomatoes, seeded and chopped
½ cup chopped sweet yellow *or* green pepper
¼ cup lightly packed fresh arugula *or* basil leaves, chopped
4 green onions, sliced (¼ cup)
¼ cup nonfat Italian salad dressing
  Nonstick spray coating
  Arugula leaves (optional)
  Lemon (optional)

Thaw fish, if frozen. Measure thickness of fish. Cut fish into serving-size pieces. For salsa, in a medium mixing bowl combine tomatoes, pepper, arugula or basil, green onion, and *2 tablespoons* of the Italian dressing.

Spray the unheated rack of a broiler pan with nonstick spray coating. Place fish on rack. Brush fish with some of the remaining Italian dressing.

Broil 4 inches from the heat till fish flakes easily with a fork. Allow 4 to 6 minutes per ½-inch thickness of fish, turning and brushing fish with the remaining dressing once.

Transfer fish to serving plates. Spoon salsa over each serving. Garnish with additional arugula leaves and lemon, if desired. Makes 4 servings.

Nutrition Information Per Serving:
203 calories, 7 g total fat, 2 g saturated fat, 47 mg cholesterol, 264 mg sodium, 5 g carbohydrate, 1 g fiber, 29 g protein.

Arugula lends its peppery taste to this colorful salsa. Serve it at room temperature for the best flavor.

CURRIED CRAB CAKES WITH CHUTNEY TARTAR SAUCE

These crispy baked crab cakes are topped with an easy stir-together chutney sauce. Choose whichever chutney you like best.

1 **pound fresh *or* frozen lump crabmeat, drained**
½ **cup fine dry bread crumbs**
¼ **cup finely chopped green onion**
¼ **cup frozen egg product, thawed**
2 **tablespoons finely chopped celery**
1 **teaspoon curry powder**
½ **teaspoon finely shredded orange peel**
¼ **cup orange juice**
 Nonstick spray coating
 Chutney Tartar Sauce

Thaw crabmeat, if frozen. In a large bowl combine crabmeat, bread crumbs, green onion, egg product, celery, curry powder, orange peel, and orange juice. Mix well. Using hands, gently shape crab mixture into 6 patties.

Spray a shallow baking pan with nonstick spray coating. Place patties in pan. Bake in a 350° oven about 20 minutes or till the patties are lightly golden. Serve with Chutney Tartar Sauce. Serves 6.

Chutney Tartar Sauce: Stir together ¼ cup *plain nonfat yogurt*, 2 tablespoons *nonfat mayonnaise dressing*, 2 tablespoons snipped *chutney*, and 1 teaspoon *balsamic vinegar or white wine vinegar*. Makes ½ cup.

Nutrition Information Per Serving: 163 calories, 3 g total fat, 0 g saturated fat, 76 mg cholesterol, 374 mg sodium, 14 g carbohydrate, 1 g fiber, 19 g protein.

FISH AND SEAFOOD BUYING GUIDE

You don't have to be a marine specialist to make smart fish and seafood choices. Here are a few easy tips to use at the fresh fish counter.

Whole Fish: Look the fish in the eyes. They should be clear and bright and not sunken. The gills should be bright red or pink, the skin should be shiny and elastic, and the scales should be tightly in place.

Fish Fillets and Steaks: Make sure the fish in the counter is displayed on a bed of ice. It should have a mild smell, not a fishy odor. Avoid fish that is dry around the edges.

Scallops: Select firm, sweet-smelling scallops in thin cloudy liquid. Don't buy scallops if they are in a thick liquid or have a strong sulfur odor.

Shrimp: Pick fresh shrimp that are moist and firm with translucent flesh and a fresh aroma. Avoid shrimp with an ammonia-like smell.

BROILED HALIBUT WITH DILL-CAPER SAUCE

1 **pound fresh *or* frozen halibut steaks, cut ½-inch thick**
 Nonstick spray coating
2 **teaspoons olive oil *or* cooking oil**
2 **large shallots, finely chopped**
1 **clove garlic, minced**
½ **cup reduced-sodium chicken broth**
¼ **cup light dairy sour cream**
1 **tablespoon all-purpose flour**
1 **tablespoon snipped parsley**
1 **teaspoon capers, rinsed and drained**
2 **teaspoons snipped fresh dill *or* ½ teaspoon dried dillweed**
1 **lemon, quartered lengthwise**
 Fresh dill (optional)

Thaw fish, if frozen. Cut into serving-size pieces. Spray the unheated rack of a broiler pan with nonstick spray coating. Place halibut steaks on rack. Lightly brush with *1 teaspoon* of the olive oil. Broil 4 inches from the heat for 4 to 6 minutes or till fish flakes easily with a fork.

Meanwhile, for sauce, in a medium saucepan cook shallots and garlic in remaining olive oil for 2 to 3 minutes or till tender. In a small mixing bowl stir together chicken, broth, sour cream, and flour; add all at once to saucepan. Cook and stir over medium heat till thickened and bubbly. Cook and stir for 1 minute more. Stir in parsley, capers, and dill. Serve halibut with sauce. Garnish with lemon wedges and, if desired, fresh dill. Makes 4 servings.

Nutrition Information Per Serving:
182 calories, 6 g total fat, 1 g saturated fat, 38 mg cholesterol, 173 mg sodium, 5 g carbohydrate, 0 g fiber, 25 g protein.

Rich-tasting and creamy, this easy sauce also goes well with grouper, cod, or orange roughy.

SOUTHWESTERN SHRIMP AND SNAPPER STEW

A hearty seafood supper flavored with chili powder and cumin. To complete your meal serve it with Parmesan Cornbread Puffs (see page 199) and a tossed salad.

8 ounces fresh *or* frozen red snapper fillets

8 ounces fresh *or* frozen large shrimp, peeled and deveined

2 14½-ounce cans reduced-sodium stewed tomatoes, cut up

1 14½-ounce can reduced-sodium chicken broth

1 12-ounce can nonalcoholic beer

1 cup very thinly sliced carrots

1 medium onion, chopped (½ cup)

½ cup uncooked long grain rice

1 tablespoon chili powder

1 teaspoon ground cumin

½ teaspoon dried oregano, crushed

2 cloves garlic, minced

1 large green pepper chopped (1 cup)

Fresh oregano sprigs (optional)

Thaw red snapper and shrimp, if frozen. Cut fish into 1-inch pieces.

In a 4-quart Dutch oven or large saucepan combine *undrained* tomatoes, chicken broth, and non-alcoholic beer. Bring to boiling. Add carrots, onion, rice, chili powder, cumin, oregano, and garlic. Return to boiling; reduce heat. Cover and simmer about 20 minutes or till the rice and carrots are nearly tender.

Add red snapper, shrimp, and green pepper. Return to boiling; reduce heat. Cover and simmer gently for 3 to 5 minutes or till red snapper flakes with a fork and shrimp turn pink. Garnish with fresh oregano sprigs, if desired. Makes 6 servings.

Nutrition Information Per Serving:
162 calories, 1 g total fat, 0 g saturated fat, 57 mg cholesterol, 266 mg sodium, 22 g carbohydrate, 4 g fiber, 15 g protein.

SEA BASS FILLETS WITH ROASTED POTATOES AND ROSEMARY

Sea bass is a delicately flavored saltwater fish with a firm texture. You can substitute any other firm fish fillets such as red snapper, cod, orange roughy, or sea trout.

1 **pound fresh** *or* **frozen sea bass, red snapper,** *or* **other firm fish fillets, ½- to ¾-inch thick**
1 **pound small red potatoes, quartered**
   Nonstick spray coating
2 **medium tomatoes, cut into wedges**
1 **tablespoon olive oil** *or* **cooking oil**
1 **tablespoon red wine vinegar**
1½ **teaspoons snipped fresh rosemary** *or* **½ teaspoon dried rosemary, crushed**
1 **tablespoon snipped chives**
⅛ **teaspoon salt**
   Dash ground pepper

Thaw fish, if frozen. Cut into serving-size pieces. Cook potatoes in a small amount of boiling water for 5 minutes. Drain well.

Spray a 13x9x2-inch baking pan with nonstick coating. In pan mix potatoes, tomatoes, oil, vinegar, and rosemary. Bake in a 400° oven 15 to 20 minutes or till potatoes are tender, stirring once. Add fish to potato mixture. Top with chives, salt, and pepper. Bake 6 to 8 minutes more or till fish flakes with a fork. Makes 4 servings.

Nutrition Information Per Serving: 274 calories, 6 g total fat, 1 g saturated fat, 47 mg cholesterol, 161 mg sodium, 30 g carbohydrate, 1 g fiber, 24 g protein.

MICROWAVE QUICK-THAW

Ooops! Forget to defrost the fish or seafood for dinner? Don't worry, just use your microwave oven and the chart below as a guide to defrosting your frozen catch. Unwrap the frozen fish or seafood and place it in a microwave-safe dish. Cover with a lid or plastic wrap and defrost on 30% power (medium-low) for the time listed below. Stir, turn, or separate the food halfway through cooking. Let it stand for a few minutes to complete thawing.

		AMOUNT	MINUTES
Fish	fillets	1 lb.	6 to 8
	steaks	1 lb.	6 to 8
Shrimp	in shells	1 lb.	6 to 8
	peeled and deveined	1 lb.	7 to 9
Scallops		1 lb.	8 to 10
Crabmeat		6 oz.	2½ to 3½

GROUPER WITH SPICY MUSTARD SAUCE

1 pound fresh *or* frozen
   grouper *or* cod fillets,
   ½-inch thick
2 tablespoons lemon juice
⅛ teaspoon cracked black
   pepper
   Nonstick spray coating
¼ cup nonfat mayonnaise
   dressing *or* salad dressing
2 tablespoons finely snipped
   chives
2 tablespoons skim milk
1 tablespoon finely snipped
   parsley
1 tablespoon capers, rinsed
   and drained
2 teaspoons Dijon-style
   mustard

Few dashes bottled hot
   pepper sauce
Chive blossoms (optional)

Thaw fish, if frozen. Cut into serving-size pieces. Sprinkle grouper fillets with lemon juice and pepper. Spray the unheated rack of a broiler pan with nonstick spray coating. Place fish on rack. Broil 4 inches from heat for 4 to 6 minutes or till fish flakes easily with a fork.

Meanwhile, for sauce, in a small mixing bowl combine mayonnaise or salad dressing, chives, skim milk, parsley, capers, Dijon-style mustard, and hot pepper sauce. Transfer fillets to serving plates. Spoon the sauce over each serving. Garnish with chive blossoms, if desired. Makes 4 servings.

Nutrition Information Per Serving:
108 calories, 1 g total fat, 0 g saturated fat, 45 mg cholesterol, 359 mg sodium, 4 g carbohydrate, 0 g fiber, 19 g protein.

If you have the time to grill, then place the fish fillets on a well-greased wire basket and grill over medium-hot coals till done. Allow 4 to 6 minutes per ½-inch thickness of fish.

SPICY BROILED SHARK STEAKS

1 **pound fresh *or* frozen shark *or* swordfish steaks, ¾-inch thick**
2 **tablespoons orange juice**
2 **green onions, thinly sliced (2 tablespoons)**
2 **tablespoons chili sauce**
1 **tablespoon finely chopped gingerroot**
1 **tablespoon reduced-sodium soy sauce**
1 **teaspoon dried basil, crushed**
  Several dashes hot chili oil
  Nonstick spray coating
  Orange slices (optional)
  Fresh basil leaves (optional)

Thaw fish, if frozen. Cut into serving-size pieces. For marinade, in a shallow bowl combine orange juice, green onion, chili sauce, gingerroot, soy sauce, basil, and chili oil. Add the fish; turn to coat with marinade. Cover; marinate at room temperature for 20 minutes.

Spray the unheated rack of a broiler pan with nonstick spray coating. Drain fish, reserving marinade. Place fish on rack. Broil 4 inches from the heat for 5 minutes. Using a wide spatula, carefully turn fish over. Brush with reserved marinade. Broil for 5 to 7 minutes more or till fish flakes easily with a fork. Garnish with orange slices and basil leaves, if desired. Discard any remaining marinade. Makes 4 servings.

Nutrition Information Per Serving: 160 calories, 5 g total fat, 1 g saturated fat, 45 mg cholesterol, 342 mg sodium, 3 g carbohydrate, 0 g fiber, 23 g protein.

How do you tell when your fish is perfectly cooked? Poke the tines of a fork into the thickest portion of the fish at a 45-degree angle. Then gently twist the fork and pull up some of the flesh. It's done when the fish flakes easily with the fork.

LIME-COD KABOBS

For extra color thread both zucchini and yellow summer squash slices on the skewers.

12 ounces fresh *or* frozen cod
    steaks *or* halibut steaks
¼ cup dry white wine
¼ cup lime juice
1 tablespoon cooking oil
1 small clove garlic, minced
½ teaspoon dried basil, crushed
¼ teaspoon dried oregano,
    crushed
⅛ teaspoon salt
⅛ teaspoon pepper
1 medium zucchini, cut into
    ½-inch slices
    Nonstick spray coating

Thaw fish, if frozen. If necessary, trim off the skin. Cut the fish into 1-inch cubes.

For marinade, in a medium mixing bowl stir together wine, lime juice, oil, garlic, basil, oregano, salt, and pepper. Add fish and stir till coated. Cover and marinate at room temperature for 20 minutes, stirring gently once or twice.

Drain fish, reserving marinade. On four 9-inch-long skewers alternately thread fish cubes and zucchini. Spray the unheated rack of a broiler pan with nonstick coating. Broil kabobs 4 inches from the heat for 4 minutes. Turn kabobs over; brush with marinade. Broil about 5 minutes more or till fish flakes easily with a fork. Makes 4 servings.

Nutrition Information Per Serving: 119 calories, 4 g total fat, 1 g saturated fat, 32 mg cholesterol, 120 mg sodium, 4 g carbohydrate, 1 g fiber, 14 g protein.

SIMPLY CITRUS

Citrus fruits are wonderfully low in calories and sodium, virtually fat free, and packed with vitamin C. They have a fresh flavor and natural sweetness that can be used in endless ways. Many citrus fruits such as lemons, limes, oranges, grapefruit, tangelos, and tangerines, are available all year round but are most abundant from December to March.

The next time a recipe calls for shredded citrus peel, go ahead and shred more than you need. Place any extra shredded peel in a small airtight container, then label and freeze. It's ready when you need it and as fresh-tasting as the minute you shredded it. You can store shredded citrus peel in the freezer for up to 6 months.

Moroccan-Style Fish

12 ounces fresh *or* frozen fish
 fillets
¾ cup reduced-sodium chicken
 broth
1 tablespoon reduced-sodium
 soy sauce
2 teaspoons cornstarch
½ teaspoon five-spice powder
¼ cup mixed dried fruit bits *or*
 raisins
2 tablespoons thinly sliced
 celery
1⅓ cups boiling water
⅔ cups couscous
1 tablespoon snipped parsley
⅛ teaspoon salt
 Nonstick spray coating
1 tablespoon reduced-sodium
 soy sauce

Thaw fish, if frozen. Cut into serving-size pieces.

For sauce, in a small saucepan combine chicken broth, 1 tablespoon soy sauce, cornstarch, and five-spice powder. Stir in dried fruit bits or raisins and celery. Cook and stir sauce till thickened and bubbly. Cook and stir for 2 minutes more. Cover the sauce to keep warm.

In a medium mixing bowl combine boiling water, couscous, parsley, and salt. Cover; let stand for 5 minutes.

Meanwhile, spray a 12x7½x2-inch baking dish with nonstick coating. Measure the thickness of the fish fillets. Place fillets in baking dish. Brush fish with 1 tablespoon soy sauce.

Bake in a 450° oven till fish just flakes with a fork (allow 4 to 6 minutes per ½-inch thickness of fish). Serve fish over couscous mixture. Ladle sauce atop. Makes 4 servings.

Nutrition Information Per Serving:
219 calories, 1 g total fat, 0 g saturated fat, 32 mg cholesterol, 574 mg sodium, 32 g carbohydrate, 5 g fiber, 19 g protein.

If using frozen fish, thaw the fillets overnight in the refrigerator or thaw in your microwave oven (see tip, page 58).

MUSSELS WITH CREAMY TWO-MUSTARD SAUCE

Use your kitchen time wisely by combining the sauce ingredients first and setting aside while you prepare the mussels.

2 pounds farm-raised mussels, (about 2 dozen)*
1 large shallot, chopped
2 large cloves garlic, minced
2 teaspoons olive oil *or* cooking oil
¾ cup dry white wine
2 celery stalks, cut into ½-inch slices
1 tablespoon snipped fresh tarragon *or* 1 teaspoon dried tarragon, crushed
1 teaspoon black peppercorns
  Creamy Two-Mustard Sauce
  Fresh tarragon sprigs (optional)

Rinse mussels and remove beards. In a 4-quart Dutch oven cook shallot and garlic in oil till tender. Add wine. Bring to boiling. Stir in the mussels, celery, tarragon, and peppercorns.

Cover; return to boiling. Reduce heat. Simmer for 3 to 5 minutes or till mussels open. Stir mussels to coat with liquid. Remove from heat. Discard any mussels that have not opened.

Divide sauce between four ramekins or shallow bowls. Serve mussels with sauce. Garnish with fresh tarragon sprigs, if desired. Makes 4 servings.

*Note: Farm-raised mussels have been cleaned, but beards have not been removed.

Creamy Two-Mustard Sauce: In a small saucepan combine ⅓ cup *plain nonfat yogurt*; 3 tablespoons *nonfat mayonnaise dressing or salad dressing;* 2 teaspoons *Dijon-style mustard;* ¾ teaspoon snipped fresh or ¼ teaspoon crushed, dried *tarragon;* and 1 teaspoon *honey.* Cook over low heat for 2 to 3 minutes or till just heated through. *Do not* boil. Makes about ⅔ cup.

Nutrition Information Per Serving: 150 calories, 3 g total fat, 0 g saturated fat, 40 mg cholesterol, 568 mg sodium, 11 g carbohydrate, 1 g fiber, 13 g protein.

45

HOT TUNA SALAD NIÇOISE

For an even easier version of this main dish salad, substitute one 10-ounce can of white solid pack tuna for the fresh tuna.

12 ounces fresh *or* frozen tuna steak

¾ pound small red potatoes, quartered (about 6 potatoes)

½ pound green beans, trimmed and cut into 1½-inch pieces

4 ripe plum tomatoes, cut into quarters

¼ cup reduced-sodium chicken broth

1 tablespoon olive oil *or* cooking oil

1 tablespoon white wine vinegar

1 tablespoon lemon juice

½ teaspoon sugar

½ teaspoon dried Italian seasoning, crushed

¼ teaspoon garlic salt

1 teaspoon Dijon-style mustard

3 cups torn mixed salad greens

Thaw fish, if frozen. Cut fish into ½-inch thick, bite-size strips. Place potatoes and green beans in a steamer basket over boiling water. Cover; steam for 15 to 20 minutes or till crisp-tender. Place vegetables in a large bowl.

Meanwhile, spray a large non-stick skillet with nonstick spray coating. Place skillet over medium heat. Cook and gently stir tuna strips for 3 to 5 minutes or till opaque. Layer tuna strips and tomatoes over vegetables.

For dressing, in the same skillet combine chicken broth, oil, vinegar, lemon juice, sugar, Italian seasoning, and garlic salt. Bring just to boiling. Boil for 1 minute. Stir in Dijon-style mustard. Drizzle over tuna and vegetables. Toss gently to mix. Serve tuna mixture immediately over greens. Makes 4 servings.

Nutrition Information Per Serving: 292 calories, 9 g total fat, 2 g saturated fat, 35 mg cholesterol, 251 mg sodium, 28 g carbohydrate, 3 g fiber, 26 g protein.

CRUNCHY OVEN FRIED FISH

1 **pound fresh *or* frozen orange roughy *or* other white fish fillets, ½-inch thick**
¼ **cup all-purpose flour**
¼ **teaspoon salt**
¼ **teaspoon lemon pepper**
1 **egg white**
¼ **cup fine dry bread crumbs**
¼ **cup cornmeal**
1½ **teaspoons finely shredded lemon peel**
½ **teaspoon dried basil, crushed**

Thaw fish, if frozen. Cut into serving-size pieces. In a shallow dish combine flour, salt, and lemon pepper; set aside.

Beat egg white till frothy. Combine bread crumbs, cornmeal, lemon peel, and basil. Dip top of fish fillets into flour mixture, shaking off any excess. Then dip into egg white, then coat with bread crumb mixture.

Spray a shallow baking pan with nonstick spray coating. Place fillets in baking pan coating side up, tucking under any thin edges. Bake in a 450° oven for 6 to 12 minutes or till fish flakes easily with a fork. Makes 4 servings.

Nutrition Information Per Serving:
174 calories, 1 g total fat, 0 g saturated fat, 43 mg cholesterol, 333 mg sodium, 18 g carbohydrate, 1 g fiber, 21 g protein.

This mock fried fish tastes delicious with a little fresh lemon or lime squeezed over it. Or, you may want to try it with the Chutney Tartar Sauce on page 54.

DELECTABLE DRIED TOMATOES

They are reddish brown, shriveled looking, and come in halves, slices, and bits. This unusual sounding food is nothing but a clever disguise for the simple tomato, known as dried tomatoes. They are vine-ripened tomatoes picked at their peak of freshness, cut in half, sometimes salted, and then dried. The result is a chewy meaty tomato with a concentrated flavor.

Look for dried tomatoes in supermarkets, gourmet shops, and specialty stores. They are either dry or packed in olive oil. To rehydrate the dry tomatoes (not in oil), cover them with boiling water and let stand about 2 minutes, then drain. Or, rehydrate them according to the package directions. To use the oil-packed tomatoes, simply remove them from the oil and pat dry with paper towels.

Store the dry form in an airtight container out of direct light or in a refrigerator or freezer for up to 1 year. You can store oil-packed tomatoes in the refrigerator after opening for up to 6 months, making sure the oil covers the tomatoes.

Dried tomatoes, in any form, add a burst of flavor to sauces, salads, sandwiches, soups, and casseroles.

COLD POACHED SALMON WITH ITALIAN VEGETABLE SALAD

1 pound fresh *or* frozen
   salmon fillets, ½- to
   ¾-inch thick
½ teaspoon coarsely cracked
   black pepper
¼ teaspoon garlic powder
1½ cups water
½ cup dry white wine *or*
   reduced-sodium chicken
   broth
2 medium shallots, minced
1 large cucumber, seeded and
   cut into ½-inch chunks
1 large red *or* green sweet
   pepper, cut into ½-inch
   chunks
1 large yellow summer squash,
   cut into ½-inch chunks
1½ teaspoons snipped fresh
   oregano *or* ½ teaspoon
   dried oregano, crushed
⅓ cup reduced-sodium chicken
   broth
1 tablespoon lemon juice
1 tablespoon olive oil *or* salad
   oil
2 cloves garlic, minced
4 large lettuce leaves

Thaw fish, if frozen. Cut into serving-size pieces. Sprinkle fish fillets with cracked pepper and garlic powder, pressing seasonings gently into the fish.

In a large skillet combine water, wine, and shallots. Bring to boiling. Carefully add salmon. Return to boiling; reduce heat. Cover and simmer gently for 4 to 8 minutes or till salmon flakes easily with a fork. Remove salmon from water. Cover and chill for 4 hours or overnight.

Meanwhile, for salad, in a large mixing bowl combine cucumber, red pepper, squash, and oregano. For dressing, in a screw-top jar combine chicken broth, lemon juice, oil, and garlic. Cover and shake well. Pour dressing over vegetables; toss to coat. Cover and chill till serving time.

To serve, line 4 dinner plates with a lettuce leaf. Using a slotted spoon, arrange chilled vegetable salad on lettuce leaves. Place one fish portion alongside salad. Makes 4 servings.

Nutrition Information Per Serving:
199 calories, 7 g total fat, 1 g saturated fat, 20 mg cholesterol, 754 mg sodium, 8 g carbohydrate, 1 g fiber, 17 g protein.

This colorful, make-ahead recipe is as fresh-tasting as it looks. Be sure to seed the cucumber to prevent it from watering out in the salad.

MAKE AHEAD

BROILED SWORDFISH WITH TANGERINE AND ONION RELISH

Look for tangerines in your grocers produce bins from October through April. Choose well-shaped, brightly colored fruit without bruises or soft spots.

1 **pound fresh *or* frozen swordfish *or* halibut steaks, ¾-inch thick**
½ **cup tangerine *or* orange juice**
2 **tablespoons brown sugar**
2 **tablespoons red wine vinegar**
  Nonstick spray coating
2 **medium tangerines, peeled, seeded, and chopped**
1 **medium red onion, chopped (½ cup)**
2 **tablespoons snipped parsley**
1 **small jalapeño pepper, seeded and finely chopped, (optional)**
1 **large clove garlic, minced**
  Parsley sprigs (optional)

Thaw fish, if frozen. Cut into serving-size pieces. In a small skillet combine tangerine or orange juice, brown sugar, and vinegar. Bring mixture just to boiling; reduce heat. Simmer, uncovered, for 5 to 6 minutes or till mixture becomes syrupy, stirring often. Remove from heat.

Spray the unheated rack of a broiler pan with nonstick spray coating. Place swordfish on rack. Brush both sides of fish with *1 tablespoon* of the juice mixture. Broil 4 inches from heat for 6 to 8 minutes or till fish flakes easily with a fork.

Meanwhile, for relish, in a medium bowl, combine chopped tangerine, onion, parsley, jalapeño pepper (if desired), and garlic. Add remaining juice mixture. Toss gently to mix. Serve fish with relish. Garnish with parsley sprigs, if desired. Makes 4 servings.

Nutrition Information Per Serving:
194 calories, 5 g total fat, 1 g saturated fat, 45 mg cholesterol, 105 mg sodium, 14 g carbohydrate, 2 g fiber, 23 g protein.

SAUTÉED GARLIC SCALLOPS WITH DRIED TOMATOES

Dried tomatoes that are not packed in oil need to be rehydrated in boiling water. While the tomatoes are soaking, prepare the remaining ingredients.

1 pound fresh *or* frozen bay *or* sea scallops
6 dried tomatoes (not oil-packed)
⅓ cup boiling water
2 teaspoons cooking oil
3 large cloves garlic, minced
2 cups sliced fresh mushrooms
2 tablespoons lemon juice
2 teaspoons cornstarch
4 green onions, sliced (¼ cup)
2 tablespoons snipped parsley
½ teaspoon finely shredded lemon peel
1 9-ounce package refrigerated spinach *or* plain fettuccine
Parsley sprigs (optional)

Thaw scallops, if frozen. In a small bowl combine dried tomatoes and boiling water. Let stand 10 minutes. Drain tomatoes, reserving liquid. Cut tomatoes into julienne strips. Set aside.

Pour oil into a large nonstick skillet; preheat over medim-high heat. Cook garlic in hot oil for 15 seconds. Add mushrooms. Cook and stir for 2 minutes. Add scallops and tomatoes. Cook and stir for 2 to 3 minutes or till scallops are opaque.

Combine lemon juice and cornstarch. Add to skillet along with reserved tomato liquid, green onions, snipped parsley, and lemon peel. Cook and stir till slightly thickened and bubbly; cook and stir for 1 minute more.

Meanwhile, cook pasta according to package directions. Drain. Serve scallop mixture over hot pasta. Garnish with parsley sprigs, if desired. Makes 4 servings.

Nutrition Information Per Serving:
215 calories, 4 g total fat, 1 g saturated fat, 55 mg cholesterol, 316 mg sodium, 26 g carbohydrate, 2 g fiber, 20 g protein.

SWEET SCALLOPS

You can treat yourself to the sweet taste of scallops all year round. And they won't sabotage your healthy eating plans since they are relatively low in fat and weigh in at only 100 calories for a 3-ounce poached serving.

There are usually three types of scallops available. Sea scallops are the largest, followed by Bay scallops and Calico scallops. The meat of these morsels can be creamy white, tan, or creamy pink.

Scallops are usually shucked right after harvest and are sold fresh or frozen.

Choose scallops that are firm and free of cloudy liquid and have a sweet aroma. Spoiled scallops have a strong sulfur odor.

Store fresh scallops in the refrigerator covered with their own liquid in a covered container for up to 2 days.

Keep scallops as healthy and fresh-tasting as possible by cooking them in little or no oil or fat. Try them broiled, poached, grilled, stir-fried, or panfried.

CREAMY HERBED FISH AND CLAM CHOWDER

12 ounces fresh *or* frozen cod fillets, cut into 1-inch pieces
2 medium potatoes, cut into cubes (about 2 cups)
½ of a 10-ounce package frozen whole kernel corn (1 cup)
1 small leek, thinly sliced
1 8-ounce bottle clam juice
¼ cup water
1 teaspoon snipped fresh thyme *or* ¼ teaspoon dried thyme, crushed
¼ teaspoon salt
⅛ teaspoon pepper

1 12-ounce can evaporated skim milk
1 6-ounce can minced clams
Fresh thyme sprigs (optional)

In a large saucepan combine potatoes, corn, leek, clam juice, water, thyme, salt, and pepper. Bring to boiling; reduce heat. Cover and simmer about 10 minutes or till potatoes are just tender.

Stir in milk. Add fish and *undrained* clams. Return to almost boiling; reduce heat. Cover and simmer for 3 to 4 minutes or till fish flakes easily with a fork. *Do not* boil. Garnish with fresh thyme, if desired. Makes 4 servings.

Nutrition Information Per Serving: 240 calories, 1 g total fat, 0 g saturated fat, 38 mg cholesterol, 534 mg sodium, 34 g carbohydrate, 3 g fiber, 24 g protein.

Evaporated skim milk gives this creamy chowder extra richness. Look for it in the baking aisle near the regular evaporated milk.

LAKE TROUT WITH CORN SALSA

Ask your butcher to skin the lake trout before you bring it home. If you opt to cook it with the skin on, then place the fish, skin side down, in the baking dish.

1 pound fresh *or* frozen lake trout *or* walleye fillets, ½-inch thick
1 cup frozen whole kernel corn
¼ cup water
½ cup small cherry tomatoes, halved
½ cup finely chopped, peeled jicama
¼ cup snipped fresh cilantro *or* parsley
2 tablespoons lime juice
1 small jalapeño pepper, seeded and finely chopped
Dash salt
Nonstick spray coating
3 tablespoons nonfat Italian salad dressing
1 teaspoon chili powder

Thaw fish, if frozen. Cut into 4 serving-size pieces.

In a small saucepan combine corn and water. Bring to boiling; reduce heat. Cover and simmer for 5 minutes; drain.

For corn salsa, in a medium serving bowl combine corn, tomatoes, jicama, cilantro or parsley, lime juice, jalapeño pepper, and salt. Toss to mix. Set aside.

Spray a 2-quart rectangular baking dish with nonstick spray coating. Stir together Italian salad dressing and chili powder; brush over fish. Place fish in the prepared baking dish. Bake, uncovered, in a 450° oven for 8 to 12 minutes or till fish flakes easily with a fork. Serve fish with corn salsa. Makes 4 servings.

Nutrition Information Per Serving: 157 calories, 1 g total fat, 0 g saturated fat, 45 mg cholesterol, 196 mg sodium, 13 g carbohydrate, 1 g fiber, 24 g protein.

BAKED RED SNAPPER WITH LEMON AND MINT

1 **pound fresh** *or* **frozen red snapper fillets, ¾- to 1-inch thick**
⅛ **teaspoon salt**
⅛ **teaspoon pepper**
1 **tablespoon snipped fresh mint** *or* **½ teaspoon dried mint, crushed**
1 **teaspoon finely shredded lemon peel**
2 **tablespoons lemon juice**

Thaw fish, if frozen. Measure thickness of fish. Place in an ungreased 2-quart rectangular baking dish, turning under thin edges to make even thickness. Season with salt and pepper. Sprinkle with mint and lemon peel.

Bake, uncovered, in a 450° oven till fish flakes easily with a fork. Allow 4 to 6 minutes per ½-inch thickness of fish. Using a slotted spatula, transfer fish fillets to a serving platter. Drizzle fish with lemon juice. Makes 4 servings.

Nutrition Information Per Serving:
116 calories, 2 g total fat, 0 g saturated fat, 42 mg cholesterol, 117 mg sodium, 1 g carbohydrate, 0 g fiber, 23 g protein.

Simple and quick, this fish is on the table in only 15 minutes. Be sure to preheat your oven while you prepare the fish for baking.

OLD MacDONALD HAD A FISH?

It's not as strange as it sounds, thanks to aquaculture. Aquaculture means raising fish and shellfish in a controlled environment. The fish and shellfish hatch, feed, and stay disease-free in pens, ponds, or tanks until they show up at the fish counter. And that's good news for you because it means greater availability of high-quality fish and seafood at lower prices.

Catfish, salmon, and trout lead the market so far, followed by hybrid striped bass, redfish, mussels, clams, oysters, crawfish, shrimp, sturgeon, and tilapia (a mild-flavored white fish). These farm-raised fish are generally milder tasting than their wild counterparts since they eat a consistent and controlled diet.

If you're unsure whether the fish and seafood you're buying has ever seen the sea, ask the person selling the fish.

ROASTED RED SNAPPER WITH TOMATOES AND FETA CHEESE

Feta cheese is a crumbly white cheese with a sharp, salty flavor. If you are watching your sodium, you can place it in a colander and rinse it under cold water to remove some of the salt.

1 pound fresh *or* frozen red snapper fillets, about 1-inch thick

1 14½-ounce can reduced-sodium tomatoes, cut up

8 green onions, sliced (½ cup)

¼ cup thinly sliced celery

2 tablespoons lemon juice

1 teaspoon dried oregano, crushed

Nonstick spray coating

¼ teaspoon pepper

¼ teaspoon ground coriander

2 tablespoons sliced ripe olives

¼ cup crumbled feta cheese (1 ounce)

Parsley sprigs (optional)

Thaw fish, if frozen. Cut into 4 serving-size portions.

For sauce, in a large skillet combine tomatoes, green onions, celery, lemon juice, and oregano. Bring to boiling; reduce heat. Simmer, uncovered, about 15 minutes or till most of the liquid has evaporated.

Meanwhile spray a 2-quart rectangular baking dish with nonstick spray coating. Place the fish in the dish, tucking under any thin edges. Sprinkle with the pepper and coriander.

Bake, uncovered, in a 450º oven for 8 to 10 minutes or till fish flakes easily with a fork.

Transfer fish to individual serving plates. Spoon sauce over fish. Sprinkle feta cheese and olives over fillets. Garnish with parsley, if desired. Makes 4 servings.

Nutrition Information Per Serving: 169 calories, 4 g total fat, 2 g saturated fat, 48 mg cholesterol, 189 mg sodium, 7 g carbohydrate, 1 g fiber, 26 g protein.

POACHED PIKE ON SPINACH WITH RED PEPPER SAUCE

1 **pound fresh *or* frozen skinless pike fillets, about ½-inch thick**

½ **cup water**

½ **cup dry white wine *or* bottled clam juice**

½ **of a 12-ounce jar roasted whole sweet red peppers, rinsed and drained (about 1 cup)**

¼ **cup lightly packed fresh parsley**

1 **tablespoon fresh lemon juice**

1 **tablespoon olive oil *or* cooking oil**

2 **teaspoons anchovy paste**

6 **cups packaged cleaned spinach**

Thaw fish, if frozen. Cut into serving-size pieces. In a large skillet combine water and wine. Bring just to boiling. Add fish. Return just to boiling; reduce heat. Cover and simmer gently for 4 to 6 minutes or till the fish flakes easily with a fork.

Meanwhile, in a food processor bowl or blender container combine roasted red peppers, parsley, lemon juice, oil, and anchovy paste. Cover and blend or process till nearly smooth. Place sauce in small saucepan. Cook over low heat to heat through.

Remove fish from skillet with slotted spatula. Arrange spinach on serving plates. Place fish on spinach. Spoon pepper sauce atop fillets. Makes 4 servings.

Nutrition Information Per Serving: 179 calories, 5 g total fat, 1 g saturated fat, 48 mg cholesterol, 261 mg sodium, 6 g carbohydrate, 3 g fiber, 26 g protein.

Pike is a freshwater fish with a firm texture and a mild flavor. If you can't find pike, try cod, orange roughy, or whitefish.

COD PRIMAVERA WITH PASTA

Want to save more time? Then buy 2 cups broccoli flowerets and 1 cup thinly sliced yellow squash at your grocer's salad bar.

¾ **pound fresh *or* frozen cod *or* other fish fillets**

2 **cups broccoli flowerets**

1 **small yellow summer squash *or* zucchini, thinly sliced (1 cup)**

1 **cup frozen peas**

4 **ounces refrigerated spinach fettuccine**

¾ **cup reduced-sodium chicken broth**

⅓ **cup dry white wine**

2 **tablespoons cornstarch**

¼ **teaspoon dried thyme, crushed**

⅛ **teaspoon pepper**

1 **medium tomato, seeded and chopped**

2 **tablespoons grated Parmesan cheese**

Thaw fish, if frozen. Cut into 1-inch pieces. Place broccoli and squash in a steamer basket set over boiling water. Cover and steam for 3 minutes. Add peas to steamer basket. Cover and steam for 3 to 4 minutes more or till vegetables are crisp-tender. Remove steamer basket from pan.

Cook pasta according to package directions except omit salt.

Meanwhile for sauce, in a medium saucepan combine chicken broth, wine, cornstarch, thyme, and pepper. Cook and stir till thickened and bubbly. Add fish. Cook for 3 to 5 minutes more or till fish flakes easily with a fork, stirring gently once or twice.

Drain pasta and return it to pan. Add vegetables. Toss gently to mix. Transfer to serving dish. Pour sauce over pasta mixture. Sprinkle with tomato and Parmesan cheese. Makes 4 servings.

Nutrition Information Per Serving: 261 calories, 3 g total fat, 1 g saturated fat, 61 mg cholesterol, 236 mg sodium, 33 g carbohydrate, 5 g fiber, 23 g protein.

SOLE WITH SPINACH AND PLUM TOMATOES

1 **pound fresh** *or* **frozen skinless sole, flounder,** *or* **whitefish fillets**

1 **10-ounce package frozen chopped spinach, thawed and well-drained**

1 **small onion, finely chopped (⅓ cup)**

2 **tablespoons snipped parsley**

2 **cloves garlic, minced**

1½ **teaspoons snipped fresh oregano** *or* **½ teaspoon dried oregano, crushed**

½ **teaspoon finely shredded orange peel**

¼ **teaspoon salt**

¼ **teaspoon pepper**

2 **plum tomatoes, chopped**

Thaw fish fillets, if frozen. Cut fish into serving-size portions.

Stir together spinach, onion, parsley, garlic, oregano, and orange peel. Place *one-fourth* of the spinach mixture in each of *four* individual casseroles. Place one fish portion in each casserole. Sprinkle fish with salt and pepper. Cover casseroles with foil.

Bake in a 400° oven 5 minutes. Remove foil. Sprinkle with tomato. Bake, uncovered, 5 to 7 minutes more or till fish flakes easily with a fork. Makes 4 servings.

Nutrition Information Per Serving: 139 calories, 2 g total fat, 0 g saturated fat, 60 mg cholesterol, 291 mg sodium, 7 g carbohydrate, 2 g fiber, 24 g protein.

Here's how to make dinner guests feel special. Each colorful serving bakes in an individual casserole to place before each guest.

HERB BASICS

Like an artists' paintbrush, herbs can color the simplest of foods and bring new life to an ordinary dish. So treat them with the respect they deserve by following some simple guidelines.

Store dried herbs in tightly covered containers in a dark place to protect them from air and light. Do not freeze dried herbs or store them near hot appliances. Replace dried herbs about once a year or whenever their aroma becomes weak.

To use a dried herb, first measure it, place it in the palm of your hand, and crush it with your other hand to release its flavor.

Don't overlook fresh herbs which are available in most supermarkets year-round and add a refreshing taste to foods. Use about three times as much fresh herb as dried (1½ teaspoons fresh snipped herb instead of ½ teaspoon dried herb). When cooking with herbs, add dried herbs at the beginning of cooking to draw out their flavors and add fresh herbs at the end of cooking to retain their fresh flavors.

FISH FILLETS AND CAPONATA-STYLE VEGETABLES

Cod topped with a chunky sauce of summer vegetables–eggplant, sweet peppers, and tomatoes, seasoned with a little oregano, makes a perfect warm weather dinner entrée.

12 **ounces fresh *or* frozen fish fillets, such as cod, haddock, *or* orange roughy**
Nonstick spray coating
½ **of a small eggplant, peeled and chopped (about 1½ cups)**
1 **small red *or* green sweet pepper, chopped (½ cup)**
1 **small onion, chopped (⅓ cup)**
1 **clove garlic, minced**
1 **small tomato, chopped**
¼ **cup water**
½ **teaspoon dried oregano *or* basil, crushed**
2 **tablespoons nonfat Italian salad dressing**
4 **½-inch thick slices French bread, toasted**
Basil leaves (optional)

Thaw fish, if frozen. Cut into serving-size pieces. Spray a large nonstick skillet with nonstick spray coating. Preheat over medium heat. Add eggplant, sweet pepper, onion, and garlic. Cook and stir for 4 minutes. Add tomato, water, oregano, and basil. Cover and cook for 1 to 2 minutes more or till vegetables are tender. Remove from heat. Stir in *1 tablespoon* of the salad dressing. Set aside.

Meanwhile, measure the thickness of fish. Spray the unheated rack of a broiler pan with nonstick spray coating. Place fish on rack. Broil 4 inches from the heat till fish flakes easily with a fork. (Allow 4 to 6 minutes per ½-inch thickness of fish.)

To assemble, drizzle bread slices with remaining 1 tablespoon salad dressing. Place one fish portion on each slice of bread. Spoon eggplant mixture over fish portions. Garnish with basil leaves, if desired. Makes 4 servings.

Nutrition Information Per Serving: 204 calories, 3 g total fat, 0 g saturated fat, 32 mg cholesterol, 351 mg sodium, 27 g carbohydrate, 4 g fiber, 18 g protein.

CATFISH AND ROASTED PEPPER SKILLET SUPPER

Using purchased roasted peppers is a great way to get that roasted pepper taste without the work. Look for jars of them alongside pickles and olives.

1 **pound fresh *or* frozen skinless catfish fillets, ½- to 1-inch thick**
1 **7-ounce jar roasted whole sweet red peppers, rinsed and drained**
 Nonstick spray coating
1 **small onion, thinly sliced**
1 **large clove garlic, minced**
1 **4-ounce can diced green chili peppers, drained**
½ **teaspoon dried Italian seasoning, crushed**

Thaw fish, if frozen. Cut into serving-size pieces. Cut roasted red peppers into strips. Spray a large nonstick skillet with nonstick spray coating. Add red pepper strips, onion, garlic, green chili peppers, and Italian seasoning. Cook over medium heat for 4 to 5 minutes or till onion is tender.

Place fish atop red pepper mixture. Reduce heat to medium-low. Cover and cook for 8 to 10 minutes or till the fish flakes easily when tested with a fork.

Using a slotted spoon or spatula, transfer fish to serving plates. Spoon *one-fourth* of the red pepper mixture over *each* serving. Makes 4 servings.

Nutrition Information Per Serving: 144 calories, 5 g total fat, 1 g saturated fat, 59 mg cholesterol, 145 mg sodium, 5 g carbohydrate, 1 g fiber, 20 g protein.

HEALTHFUL
MEAT

SMOTHERED STEAK WITH HONEYED RED ONIONS

⅓ cup red wine vinegar
3 tablespoons honey
½ teaspoon dried thyme, crushed
1 large red onion, thinly sliced
1 pound beef top loin *or* tenderloin steaks, cut 1-inch thick
½ teaspoon cracked black pepper
2 tablespoons snipped parsley
Flat-leaf parsley (optional)

In a medium bowl stir together the red wine vinegar, honey, and thyme. Separate the onion slices; add to the vinegar mixture. Let stand while preparing meat; stir occasionally.

Meanwhile, trim fat from meat; cut into serving-size pieces. Sprinkle both sides of steak with cracked pepper, pressing pepper into the surface of the meat.

In a large nonstick skillet cook steaks over medium-high heat for 10 minutes, turning once. Remove steaks from skillet.

Add the onion mixture to the drippings in skillet. Cook over medium heat for 3 to 4 minutes or till onions are just crisp-tender, stirring occasionally.

Return steaks and any accumulated juices to skillet. Reduce heat to medium-low. Cook, uncovered, for 3 to 4 minutes or till steak is desired doneness and liquid is slightly reduced, occasionally spooning the cooking liquid over the steaks. Transfer steaks to serving plates. Stir snipped parsley into onion mixture. Spoon the onion mixture over the steaks. Garnish with flat-leaf parsley, if desired. Makes 4 servings.

Nutrition Information Per Serving:
273 calories, 10 g total fat, 4 g saturated fat, 76 mg cholesterol, 59 mg sodium, 19 g carbohydrate, 1 g fiber, 26 g protein.

Another time, substitute a sweet onion variety, such as Vidalia or Walla Walla for the red onion in the sweet-and-sour relish that tops these steaks.

MEAT PATTIES WITH MUSHROOM-WINE SAUCE

Look for 8-ounce packages of pre-sliced fresh mushrooms alongside whole mushrooms. Chances are they won't cost any more than the packages of whole mushrooms.

1 **beaten egg white**
¼ **cup skim milk**
¾ **cup soft bread crumbs**
¼ **cup snipped parsley**
¼ **cup chopped fresh mushrooms**
2 **small shallots, minced**
2 **cloves garlic, minced**
1½ **teaspoons snipped fresh thyme** *or* **½ teaspoon dried thyme, crushed**
8 **ounces 90% lean ground beef**
8 **ounces ground raw chicken** *or* **turkey**
½ **cup reduced-sodium chicken broth**
1 **cup sliced fresh mushrooms**
2 **green onions, thinly sliced**
1 **tablespoon dry white wine**

In a mixing bowl combine egg white and milk. Stir in bread crumbs, parsley, chopped mushrooms, shallots, garlic, and thyme. Add beef and chicken or turkey; mix well. Shape meat mixture into six 4-inch patties.

Place patties on the unheated rack of a broiler pan. Broil 3 to 4 inches from the heat for 15 to 18 minutes or till no pink remains, turning patties once.

Meanwhile, for sauce, in a medium skillet combine chicken broth, sliced mushrooms, green onions, and white wine. Bring to boiling. Boil for 5 to 6 minutes or till sauce is reduced by about half. Serve the sauce over the meat patties. Makes 6 servings.

Nutrition Information Per Serving: 146 calories, 7 g total fat, 2 g saturated fat, 42 mg cholesterol, 137 mg sodium, 5 g carbohydrate, 0 g fiber, 15 g protein.

LOOK FOR LEAN

Cooking with the leanest ground beef available helps keep your fat and cholesterol intake low. Look for 90 percent lean (10 percent fat) on the ground beef package. In some areas of the country, you can buy beef as lean as 95 percent. This low-fat meat has some of the fat replaced with water and plant-derived ingredients to maintain moisture during cooking. No matter which type you choose, be sure to drain the fat well after cooking to ensure your recipe will be as low-fat as possible.

ORIENTAL PEPPER STEAK

12 ounces lean beef sirloin steak
¼ cup reduced-sodium beef
   broth
2 tablespoons reduced-sodium
   soy sauce
2 tablespoons dry sherry *or*
   water
2 teaspoons cornstarch
1 teaspoon toasted seame oil
½ to 1 teaspoon crushed red
   pepper
½ teaspoon ground coriander
¼ teaspoon ground ginger
2 teaspoons cooking oil
2 cloves garlic, minced
4 cups sliced bok choy
1 large red, green, *and /or*
   yellow sweet pepper,
   cut into strips (1½ cups)
2 cups hot cooked rice

Trim fat from beef. Thinly slice beef across the grain into bite-size strips. For sauce, in a small bowl stir together beef broth, soy sauce, sherry, cornstarch, sesame oil, crushed red pepper, coriander, and ginger. Set sauce aside.

Add *1 teaspoon* of the cooking oil to a wok or large nonstick skillet. Preheat over medium-high heat. Add garlic; stir-fry for 15 seconds. Add bok choy; stir-fry for 1 minute. Add pepper strips; stir-fry for 2 to 3 minutes more or till the vegetables are crisp-tender. Remove the vegetables from the wok or skillet.

Add remaining 1 teaspoon oil to wok. Add beef; stir-fry for 2 to 3 minutes more or till desired doneness. Push beef from center of wok. Stir sauce; add to center of wok. Cook and stir till thickened and bubbly. Return vegetables to wok. Stir vegetables to coat with sauce. Cook about 2 minutes more or till heated through. Serve with rice. Makes 4 servings.

Nutrition Information Per Serving: 358 calories, 12 g total fat, 4 g saturated fat, 57 mg cholesterol, 359 mg sodium, 36 g carbohydrate, 2 g fiber, 24 g protein.

This sizzling sirloin dish uses bok choy which is a variety of Chinese cabbage with long white stalks and large deep green leaves. Use both the stalks and leaves in this peppery recipe.

MEDITERRANEAN-STYLE BEEF STIR-FRY

You'll have no problem making this in 30 minutes or less if you start heating the water for the pasta before cutting up the ingredients.

12 ounces boneless beef top round steaks, cut ¾-inch thick
Nonstick spray coating
2 cloves garlic, minced
1 medium yellow summer squash, halved and sliced diagonally
2 cups fresh *or* frozen broccoli flowerets
1 teaspoon cooking oil
1 cup cherry tomato halves
⅓ cup reduced-calorie *or* nonfat Italian salad dressing
4 green onions, thinly sliced (¼ cup)
6 ounces fettuccine *or* linguine, cooked and drained
1 tablespoon finely shredded Parmesan cheese

Trim fat from beef. Thinly slice beef across the grain into bite-size strips. Spray a wok or large nonstick skillet with nonstick spray coating. Heat over medium heat. Stir-fry garlic for 15 seconds. Add squash and broccoli; stir-fry for 4 to 5 minutes or till crisp-tender.

Remove from wok. Add oil to wok. Add beef to wok; stir-fry for 3 to 4 minutes or till desired doneness. Return vegetables to wok. Add cherry tomato halves, salad dressing, and green onions. Toss to mix. Cover and heat through. Serve beef mixture over hot pasta. Sprinkle with Parmesan cheese. Makes 4 servings.

Nutrition Information Per Serving: 371 calories, 9 g total fat, 2 g saturated fat, 57 mg cholesterol, 251 mg sodium, 43 g carbohydrate, 4 g fiber, 30 g protein.

ORANGE-GLAZED STEAK

Just because you use a small amount of frozen orange juice concentrate doesn't mean you have to thaw it and use the remaining concentrate right away. Just cover the can and put it back in the freezer till you're ready to use it again.

1 tablespoon frozen orange juice concentrate, thawed
1 tablespoon water
½ teaspoon dried basil, crushed
¼ teaspoon garlic powder
⅛ teaspoon salt
⅛ teaspoon pepper
1 pound boneless beef top sirloin steak

In a small bowl combine orange juice concentrate, water, basil, garlic powder, salt, and pepper.

Trim fat from beef. Place beef on the unheated rack of a broiler pan. Brush with some of the juice mixture. Broil about 4 inches from the heat for 8 minutes. Brush with juice mixture; turn and brush again. Broil for 8 to 10 minutes more or till desired doneness, brushing once with the remaining juice mixture. Slice steak to serve. Makes 4 servings.

Nutrition Information Per Serving: 209 calories, 10 g total fat, 4 g saturated fat, 76 mg cholesterol, 123 mg sodium, 2 g carbohydrate, 0 g fiber, 26 g protein.

MICROWAVE QUICK-THAW

Ooops! Forget to defrost the meat for tonight's dinner? Don't worry, as long as you have a microwave oven. Use the chart below as a guide to defrosting your frozen meat.

Before you begin, unwrap the frozen meat and place it in a microwave-safe dish. Cover with a lid or plastic wrap and defrost on 30% power (medium-low) for the time listed below. Stir, turn, or separate the food halfway through cooking. Let it stand for a few minutes to complete thawing.

		Minutes per Pound
Beef	roast	5 to 6
	steak	7 to 8
	stew meat	5 to 6
	ground	7 to 8
Pork	roast	7 to 8
	steak/chop	7 to 8
	bulk sausage	6 to 7
	ground	7 to 8
Lamb	roast	5 to 6
	chop	7 to 8
	ground	7 to 8

SWISS STEAK WITH FRESH TOMATOES

2 tablespoons all-purpose flour
½ teaspoon dried oregano, crushed
¼ teaspoon dried rosemary *or* marjoram, crushed
¼ teaspoon pepper
12 ounces lean cubed steaks
   Nonstick spray coating
2 stalks celery, sliced
1 medium carrot, thinly sliced
1 large leek, sliced *or*
   1 medium onion, sliced
½ cup water
2 cloves garlic, minced
¼ teaspoon instant beef bouillon granules
2 large tomatoes, chopped
2 tablespoons dry red wine *or* water
1 tablespoon tomato paste

In a shallow dish combine flour, oregano, rosemary or marjoram, and pepper. Coat both sides of meat pieces with flour mixture.

Spray a large nonstick skillet with nonstick spray coating. Brown meat on both sides over medium heat. Add celery, carrots, leek or onion, water, garlic, and beef bouillon granules to skillet. Bring to boiling; reduce heat. Cover and simmer for 15 minutes.

Add tomatoes, wine, and tomato paste to the skillet. Cover and simmer about 2 minutes more or till the meat and vegetables are tender. Makes 4 servings.

Nutrition Information Per Serving:
189 calories, 5 g total fat, 2 g saturated fat, 54 mg cholesterol, 218 mg sodium, 13 g carbohydrate, 3 g fiber, 22 g protein.

For a change of pace, serve this fat-trimmed classic with hot cooked strands of spaghetti squash.

HOT AND SOUR THAI BEEF SALAD

The flavors of gingerroot, basil, mint, and hot peppers characterize this stir-fry salad as unmistakably Thai.

1 **large yellow, red, *or* green sweet pepper, cut into bite-size strips**

½ **of a medium cucumber, cut into bite-size strips (1 cup)**

¼ **cup lime juice**

3 **tablespoons reduced-sodium soy sauce**

2 **tablespoons brown sugar**

1 **tablespoon grated gingerroot *or* ½ teaspoon ground ginger**

1 **tablespoon snipped fresh basil *or* 1 teaspoon dried basil, crushed**

1½ **teaspoons snipped fresh mint *or* ½ teaspoon dried mint, . crushed**

12 **ounces beef top sirloin steak**

Nonstick spray coating

1 **clove garlic, minced**

1 **jalapeño pepper, seeded and minced**

4 **cups packaged mixed greens**

In a medium bowl combine sweet pepper and cucumber. For dressing, in a small bowl stir together lime juice, soy sauce, brown sugar, ground ginger (if using), basil, and mint. Set aside.

Trim fat from beef. Cut into thin bite-size strips. Spray a cold wok or large skillet with nonstick spray coating. Preheat over medium heat. Add garlic, jalapeño pepper, and gingerroot (if using). Stir-fry for 30 seconds. Add beef strips; stir-fry for 3 to 4 minutes or till desired doneness. Remove beef mixture from wok. Add to vegetable mixture. Toss gently.

Add dressing to wok. Bring to boiling; boil for 30 seconds. Remove from heat.

Divide greens among four dinner plates. Spoon beef mixture over the greens. Drizzle the dressing over all. Serve immediately. Makes 4 servings.

Nutrition Information Per Serving: 219 calories, 8 g total fat, 3 g saturated fat, 57 mg cholesterol, 468 mg sodium, 15 g carbohydrate, 1 g fiber, 22 g protein.

HOW TO HANDLE HOT CHILI PEPPERS

Hot chili peppers provide a searing zip to many recipes, but take a few precautions to make sure they don't sear you at the same time. Protect your skin from the pepper's oils by covering your hands with plastic gloves, rubber gloves, or plastic bags. If your bare hands touch the chili peppers, wash your hands and under your nails thoroughly with soap and water. Never rub your mouth, nose, eyes, or ears when working with hot peppers.

If you're still concerned about handling peppers, look for jars of chopped fresh jalepeño peppers in your supermarket's produce section near the jars of minced fresh garlic.

ROAST BEEF AND PEPPERCORN PITAS

This six-ingredient sandwich is stuffed with lean roast beef from the deli and is topped with a peppercorn coleslaw and cucumbers.

3 cups coleslaw mix (shredded cabbage with carrot)
⅓ cup nonfat peppercorn ranch salad dressing
3 tablespoons finely chopped onion
4 pita bread rounds
8 ounces thinly sliced deli roast beef
½ of a medium cucumber, thinly sliced

In a medium bowl combine the coleslaw mix, salad dressing, and the onion.

Cut pita rounds in half. Divide beef among pita halves. Add cucumber slices and about ¼ *cup* of the coleslaw mixture to each pita half. Serve immediately. Makes 8 servings.

Nutrition Information Per Serving: 132 calories, 3 g total fat, 1 g saturated fat, 22 mg cholesterol, 234 mg sodium, 15 g carbohydrate, 1 g fiber, 11 g protein.

BUYING LEAN

Many fresh meats are leaner than ever before, giving you more to choose from in the meat case. Here is a handy guide to choosing the leanest meat available.

● **Beef:** Look at both the grade and cut of beef. The three grades of beef you'll find most often are Prime, Choice, and Select. Prime contains the most fat within the meat (called marbling) and Select contains the least amount of fat. Besides the grade, choose certain cuts of meat to control the amount of fat found in meat. The leanest beef cuts are top loin steak, tenderloin roast or steak, Porterhouse or T-bone steak, bottom and top sirloin steak, top sirloin roast, top round roast, and eye of round roast and steaks.

● **Veal:** Veal is naturally lean because the meat is from young animals that have not developed much fat. As for beef, veal is graded into Prime, Choice, and Select. The leanest cuts of veal are cutlet, chops (arm, rib, or loin), shoulder arm roast and steak, round steak, and ground veal.

● **Pork:** Today's pork is 50 percent leaner than 20 years ago. The leanest cuts include boneless loin roast and chops, top loin roast, tenderloin, top loin chops, loin chops, boneless ham, and Canadian bacon.

● **Lamb:** You can spot the leanest lamb by looking for packages with a red, white, and blue Certified Fresh American Lamb stamp. The leanest cuts are from the leg and loin and include sirloin chops, boneless leg roast, whole leg, and loin chops.

BEEF SIRLOIN WITH STEAMED AUTUMN VEGETABLES

8 ounces parsnips, peeled and
   cut into ½-inch thick slices
   (2 to 3 medium)
8 ounces turnips, peeled and
   cut into ½-inch pieces
   (1 medium)
2 medium carrots, cut into
   ½-inch slices (1 cup)
12 ounces boneless beef sirloin
   or top loin steak,
   cut 1-inch thick
2 cloves garlic, minced
1 tablespoon snipped fresh
   thyme *or* 1 teaspoon dried
   thyme, crushed
1 teaspoon grated
   gingerroot
⅛ teaspoon pepper
   Dash ground cloves
¼ cup snipped chutney

Place a steamer basket in a large saucepan with ½-inch water; heat to boiling. Add parsnips, turnips, and carrots to basket; cover and steam for 12 to 15 minutes or till vegetables are crisp-tender.

Meanwhile, cut meat into 4 serving-size pieces. Combine garlic, thyme, gingerroot, pepper, and cloves; rub over both sides of meat. Place meat on the unheated rack of a broiler pan. Broil 3 to 4 inches from the heat for 8 to 12 minutes for rare or 13 to 17 minutes for medium doneness, turning meat once.

Discard the water for the vegetables and place vegetables in a bowl; add chutney, stirring to coat. Serve the vegetables with meat. Makes 4 servings.

Nutrition Information Per Serving:
260 calories, 8 g total fat, 3 g saturated fat, 57 mg cholesterol, 101 mg sodium, 27 g carbohydrate, 6 g fiber, 21 g protein.

This tasty medley of steamed parsnips, turnips, and carrots would taste equally well with lamb chops or pork loin.

GROUND PORK PATTIES WITH HERBED SWEET POTATO CHIPS

12 ounces lean ground pork (not less than 75 percent lean)
2 green onions, finely chopped (2 tablespoons)
¼ teaspoon seasoned salt
¼ teaspoon pepper
½ cup apple juice
2 tablespoons coarse-grain brown mustard
1 tablespoon brown sugar
1 teaspoon cornstarch
½ teaspoon dried sage, crushed
3 cups shredded lettuce *or* spinach
  Herbed Sweet Potato Chips
  Baby pear tomatoes (optional)

In a medium bowl combine pork, green onion, seasoned salt, and pepper. Shape meat mixture into four ½-inch thick patties.

In a large skillet cook patties over medium heat for 5 minutes. Turn and cook for 5 minutes more. Pour off any drippings.

Meanwhile, for sauce, in a small saucepan combine apple juice, mustard, brown sugar, cornstarch, and sage. Cook and stir over medium heat till thickened and bubbly. Cook and stir for 2 minutes more.

Turn patties again; brush with some of the mustard sauce. Cook for 3 to 4 minutes more or till no pink remains.

To serve, divide shredded lettuce or spinach among 4 dinner plates. Top with about *2 tablespoons* of the mustard sauce. Arrange Herbed Sweet Potato Chips on the plate. Garnish with baby pear tomatoes, if desired. Makes 4 servings.

Herbed Sweet Potato Chips: Spray a 15x10x1-inch baking pan with *nonstick spray coating*; set aside. In a large bowl combine 3 medium *sweet potatoes*, sliced ⅛ inch thick (about 1 pound); 1 tablespoon *cooking oil*; 2 teaspoons *salt-free seasoning*; and ½ teaspoon *barbecue seasoning*. Toss gently till potatoes are well coated. Spread potatoes evenly in a single layer on the prepared baking pan. Bake in a 450° oven for 12 to 15 minutes or till tender. Serve the chips immediately.

Nutrition Information Per Serving: 272 calories, 11 g total fat, 1 g saturated fat, 40 mg cholesterol, 306 mg sodium, 31 g carbohydrate, 4 g fiber, 13 g protein.

Here's a good game plan for this recipe. Mix and shape the meat patties. Then, prepare the sweet potatoes. Once the potatoes are in the oven, start cooking the patties and preparing the sauce.

GARLIC PORK BALSAMICO

Ten cloves of garlic may sound like a lot, but after cooking garlic's pungent flavor mellows to give the chops a mild, slightly sweet taste.

1 **small bulb garlic**
    (about 10 cloves)
1 **cup water**
12 **ounces boneless pork loin,**
    cut into 4 slices
1 **teaspoon dried rosemary,**
    crushed
1 **teaspoon olive oil**
¼ **cup balsamic vinegar**
2 **tablespoons water**
1 **tablespoon honey-mustard**
    Fresh rosemary sprigs
    (optional)

Separate garlic bulb into cloves. *Do not* peel. In a small saucepan combine garlic cloves and 1 cup water. Bring to boiling. Boil for 2 minutes. Drain; cool slightly. Peel cloves and set aside.

Sprinkle both sides of chops with rosemary, pressing into surface of the meat.

Heat oil in a large nonstick skillet. Cook pork and garlic cloves over medium heat for 10 to 12 minutes or till no pink remains and juices run clear, turning meat over after half the cooking time. Remove the pork, leaving the garlic cloves in the skillet. Keep the pork warm.

For sauce, stir together vinegar, 2 tablespoons water, and honey-mustard. Add to garlic in skillet, stirring to scrape up any browned bits. Bring mixture just to boiling. Reduce heat. Simmer for 1 to 2 minutes or till sauce becomes slightly thickened. To serve, spoon sauce over chops. Garnish with fresh rosemary sprigs, if desired. Makes 4 servings.

Nutrition Information Per Serving:
143 calories, 7 g total fat, 2 g saturated fat, 38 mg cholesterol, 128 mg sodium, 6 g carbohydrate, 0 g fiber, 13 g protein.

PORK WITH PEAR-PEPPERCORN SAUCE

These sizzling pork chops are sauced with a harmonious mixture of sweet pear juice, mustard, nutmeg, and freshly ground pepper.

2 medium pears, cored and sliced
  Pear nectar *or* orange juice (about 1 cup)
1 tablespoon cooking oil
4 3-ounce boneless pork loin chops, cut 1 inch thick (America's Cut)
1 tablespoon all-purpose flour
1 tablespoon Dijon-style mustard
1 teaspoon whole black *or* multicolored peppercorns, crushed
¼ teaspoon ground nutmeg

In a medium saucepan cook pear slices, covered, in *1 cup* pear nectar or orange juice for 5 to 7 minutes or till tender. Remove with a slotted spoon, reserving liquid. Cover pears; keep warm.

Measure liquid, and if necessary, add additional pear nectar or orange juice to equal 1 cup. Set liquid aside.

In a large skillet heat cooking oil over medium-high heat. Add pork; reduce heat to medium.

Cook, uncovered, for 10 to 12 minutes or till no pink remains and juices run clear, turning once during cooking. Remove chops from skillet and keep warm, reserving the drippings in the skillet.

For the sauce, stir flour into the reserved drippings. Stir in the 1 cup reserved nectar, mustard, peppercorns, and nutmeg. Cook and stir till thickened and bubbly. Cook and stir for 1 minute more.

To serve, place chops on individual plates; arrange pears around chops. Top with sauce; sprinkle with additional crushed pepper, if desired. Makes 4 servings.

Nutrition Information Per Serving:
231 calories, 10 g total fat, 2 g saturated fat, 38 mg cholesterol, 127 mg sodium, 24 g carbohydrate, 3 g fiber, 13 g protein.

WARM SALAD OF PORK AND BLACK-EYED PEAS

1 **10-ounce package frozen black-eyed peas *or* one 15-ounce can black-eyed peas, rinsed and drained**
⅓ **cup nonfat Italian salad dressing**
2 **green onions, sliced (¼ cup)**
¼ **cup sliced fresh mushrooms**
¼ **cup sliced celery**
2 **tablespoons chopped pimiento**
2 **tablespoons sliced pitted ripe olives**
2 **cloves garlic, minced**
½ **pound pork tenderloin, cut into thin strips**
3 **cups spinach leaves**

If using frozen peas, cook according to package directions; drain. In a medium mixing bowl combine the black-eyed peas, salad dressing, green onion, mushrooms, celery, pimiento, and the olives; set the mixture aside.

Spray a large skillet with nonstick spray coating. Heat over medium heat. Add garlic; stir-fry for 30 seconds. Add pork; stir-fry for 2 to 3 minutes or till no pink remains. Remove from heat. Add the vegetable mixture to the pork in the skillet; mix well. Serve immediately on spinach-lined plates. Makes 3 servings.

Nutrition Information Per Serving: 285 calories, 5 g total fat, 1 g saturated fat, 54 mg cholesterol, 502 mg sodium, 33 g carbohydrate, 9 g fiber, 29 g protein.

Black-eyed peas, also called cowpeas, give this fiber-rich salad a satisfying earthy flavor. Choose between the convenience of frozen or canned peas. Remember, the canned peas contain additional sodium.

FRESHNESS AT THE MEAT MARKET

The best recipes start with the freshest ingredients, and that goes for meat, too. Here are a few fresh tips to use when buying meat.

● Beef: Check the color. Fresh beef should be bright red to deep red. Avoid beef that has any gray or brown patches and an off odor.

● Lamb: Lamb should have a pinkish red color and a thin layer of firm, white fat surrounding it.

● Pork: Fresh pork should be light pink. Smoked pork will be a slightly darker shade of pink and more firm than fresh.

● Ham: Look for rosy pink ham with a finely grained texture. Iridescence on the surface of ham does not affect quality. Press the ham gently to make sure it feels firm and not spongy.

PORK SALAD WITH CABBAGE SLAW

The time-saving secret to this recipe is to use preshredded coleslaw mix found in your supermarket produce section.

2 boneless pork loin chops, cut 1¼-inches thick (America's Cut)
¼ teaspoon cracked black pepper
⅛ teaspoon ground nutmeg
2 slices turkey bacon *or* bacon
5 cups coleslaw mix (shredded cabbage with carrot)
1 cup coarsely chopped apple
⅓ cup cider vinegar
⅓ cup apple juice
1 tablespoon honey
2 teaspoons honey-mustard
1 teaspoon caraway seed
Apple slices (optional)

Sprinkle pork with pepper and nutmeg. Place meat on the unheated rack of a broiler pan. Broil 4 to 5 inches from the heat for 18 to 25 minutes or till no pink remains and juices run clear, turning the meat once during cooking.

Meanwhile, in a large bowl combine coleslaw mix and apple; set aside. In a medium skillet cook bacon slices till crisp. Drain. Crumble bacon; set aside.

Add vinegar, apple juice, honey, mustard, and caraway seed to skillet. Bring to boiling.

Pour over coleslaw mixture; add crumbled bacon. Toss to mix. Arrange coleslaw mixture on individual serving plates. Cut pork into ¼-inch thick slices. Arrange pork slices on coleslaw mixture. Garnish with apple slices, if desired. Makes 4 servings.

Nutrition Information Per Serving: 167 calories, 6 g total fat, 2 g saturated fat, 30 mg cholesterol, 212 mg sodium, 20 g carbohydrate, 3 g fiber, 11 g protein.

ORANGE BASIL PORK MEDAILLONS

Meat medaillons are slices of meat that are typically pounded with a meat mallet to about ½-inch thickness. To keep these pork medaillons tender and juicy, cook them only until there is a little pink left.

⅔ **cup couscous**
1 **cup orange juice**
¼ **cup water**
2 **teaspoons cornstarch**
1 **teaspoon instant chicken bouillon granules**
½ **teaspoon dried basil, crushed**
⅛ **teaspoon pepper**
12 **ounces pork tenderloin**
  Nonstick spray coating
1 **tablespoon snipped parsley**
  Orange peel strips
    (optional)

Prepare couscous according to package directions.

For sauce, in a small bowl stir together orange juice, water, cornstarch, bouillon granules, basil, and pepper. Set aside.

Cut pork into 12 equal slices. Place each slice of pork between two sheets of plastic wrap. Lightly pound the slices with the flat side of the meat mallet to about ½-inch thickness.

Spray a cold large skillet with nonstick spray coating. Preheat over medium heat. Add pork slices to the skillet. Cook over medium heat for 3 minutes. Turn slices over and cook about 2 minutes more or till just slightly pink. Remove the pork from the skillet; keep warm.

Stir sauce; add sauce to the skillet. Cook and stir over medium heat till thickened and bubbly. Cook and stir for 1 minute more. Stir parsley into couscous. Arrange couscous and pork on a serving platter. Garnish with orange peel strips, if desired. Makes 4 servings.

Nutrition information per serving:
261 calories, 4 g total fat, 1 g saturated fat, 61 mg cholesterol, 265 mg sodium, 31 g carbohydrate, 5 g fiber, 23 g protein.

LEMONY MOZZARELLA AND VEGETABLE-STUFFED VEAL ROLLS

8 to 12 asparagus spears
1 pound veal top round steak,
  cut ¼-inch thick
1½ ounces part-skim mozzarella
  cheese
½ of a small red *or* yellow sweet
  pepper, cut into
  8 to 12 very thin strips
1 tablespoon snipped fresh
  basil *or* 1 teaspoon dried
  basil, crushed
1 teaspoon lemon pepper
  seasoning
1 teaspoon finely shredded
  lemon peel
1 clove garlic, minced
  Nonstick spray coating
2 tablespoons lemon juice
  Fresh basil leaves
  (optional)

Trim asparagus to about 4 inches in length. Cook asparagus, covered, in a small amount of boiling water for 1 to 2 minutes or till crisp-tender. Drain and rinse under cold water. Set aside.

Cut veal into 4 pieces. Place each piece of veal between two sheets of plastic wrap. Lightly pound the meat with the flat side of a meat mallet to ⅛-inch thickness. Cut the cheese into 4 strips.

Place 2 to 3 asparagus spears, 2 to 3 sweet pepper strips, and 1 piece of cheese onto one end of each piece of veal. Roll up, tucking in ends as you roll. Secure with a wooden pick.

In a small bowl combine basil, lemon pepper seasoning, lemon peel, and garlic. Rub mixture evenly over meat rolls. Spray a large skillet with nonstick spray coating. Heat over medium heat. Cook meat rolls for 2 to 3 minutes, turning to brown evenly. Add lemon juice to skillet. Reduce heat to medium-low. Cover and simmer for 8 to 10 minutes or till juices run clear. Transfer veal rolls to serving plates. Garnish with fresh basil, if desired. Makes 4 servings.

Nutrition Information Per Serving:
194 calories, 7 g total fat, 3 g saturated fat, 98 mg cholesterol, 389 mg sodium, 3 g carbohydrate, 1 g fiber, 29 g protein.

Make this company-special veal in the spring when asparagus is at its best. If you can't wait till spring, then use frozen asparagus spears instead of fresh.

ITALIAN VEAL STEW WITH POLENTA

Nonstick spray coating
1 **medium onion, cut into wedges**
1 **medium green pepper, coarsely chopped**
2 **cloves garlic, minced**
1 **14½-ounce can reduced-sodium whole tomatoes, cut up**
¼ **cup dry red wine**
1 **teaspoon instant chicken bouillon granules**
1 **teaspoon dried Italian seasoning, crushed**
12 **ounces boneless veal round steak, cut ½-inch thick**
2¾ **cups water**
⅛ **teaspoon salt**
¾ **cup instant polenta**
2 **cups torn spinach**
Parsley sprigs (optional)

Spray a large saucepan with nonstick spray coating. Heat over medium heat. Add onion, pepper, and garlic. Cook, for 4 to 5 minutes or till vegetables are just tender, stirring occasionally. Add tomatoes, wine, bouillon granules, and Italian seasoning. Bring to boiling; reduce heat. Cover and simmer for 10 minutes.

Meanwhile, cut veal into bite-size strips. Spray a large nonstick skillet with nonstick spray coating. Heat over medum heat. Add veal strips and stir-fry about 4 minutes or till no pink remains.

In a 2-quart saucepan heat the water and salt to boiling. Stir in polenta. Cook stirring frequently for 5 minutes.

Add veal and spinach to tomato mixture; heat through. To serve, spoon polenta into shallow soup plates or bowls. Top with veal mixture. Garnish with parsley, if desired. Makes 4 servings.

By cutting the veal into thin strips instead of cubes, you can have a full-flavored stew in half an hour that tastes like it simmered all day.

Nutrition Information Per Serving:
263 calories, 4 g total fat, 1 g saturated fat, 69 mg cholesterol, 387 mg sodium, 30 g carbohydrate, 3 g fiber, 23 g protein.

VEAL SCALOPPINE WITH FENNEL AND ORANGE

Fennel, a popular vegetable in Italian cuisine, is a winter vegetable. You will generally find it available from September through April in the produce section of your supermarket.

12 ounces boneless veal leg round steak *or* veal leg sirloin steak, cut ¼-inch thick, *or* 12 ounces pork tenderloin, cut into 1-inch thick pieces

¼ teaspoon salt

¼ teaspoon pepper

3 tablespoons olive oil *or* margarine

2 small fennel bulbs, thinly sliced

1 teaspoon finely shredded orange peel

⅔ cup orange juice

2 teaspoons all-purpose flour

If using veal, cut into four pieces. Place each piece of veal or pork between two pieces of plastic wrap. With the flat side of a meat mallet, pound the veal or pork to ⅛-inch thickness. Remove the plastic wrap. Sprinkle the veal or pork with salt and pepper.

Place *1 tablespoon* of the olive oil or margarine in a large skillet. Cook half of the veal or pork in hot oil or melted margarine over medium-high heat for 3 to 4 minutes or till no pink remains, turning to brown meat evenly. Transfer the meat to a serving platter. Cover to keep warm. Repeat with 1 tablespoon oil and the remaining veal or pork. Transfer the meat to the platter; reserve the drippings in the skillet.

Cut any large fennel slices in half. Add the remaining olive oil or margarine to the hot skillet. Add fennel slices. Cook and stir over medium-high heat for 4 to 5 minutes or till the fennel is tender but not brown.

In a small mixing bowl stir together the orange peel, orange juice, and flour. Add the orange juice mixture to the cooked fennel in the skillet. Cook and stir, scraping up any browned bits, till the sauce is thickened and bubbly. Cook and stir for 1 minute more.

To serve, spoon the fennel and orange mixture over the veal or pork. Makes 4 servings.

Nutrition Information Per Serving: 228 calories, 13 g total fat, 3 g saturated fat, 69 mg cholesterol, 194 mg sodium, 7 g carbohydrate, 0 g fiber, 19 g protein.

CURRIED APPLE-GLAZED SKEWERED LAMB

2 tablespoons frozen apple
   juice concentrate, thawed
1 to 2 teaspoons curry powder
1 teaspoon grated gingerroot
¼ teaspoon garlic powder
12 ounces boneless lean lamb,
   cut into 1-inch cubes
4 to 5 green onions, cut into
   1-inch pieces
1 large red *or* green sweet
   pepper, cut into
   ¾-inch pieces
1⅓ cups boiling water
⅔ cup couscous
1 tablespoon snipped parsley

For sauce, in a small bowl combine apple juice concentrate, curry powder, gingerroot, and garlic powder. Set aside.

Spray the unheated rack of a broiler pan with nonstick spray coating. For kabobs, on four 8-inch long skewers, alternately thread lamb, green onion, and red or green pepper. Place kabobs on rack. Brush with sauce. Broil 3 inches from heat for 6 to 8 minutes or till lamb is desired doneness, turning occasionally.

Meanwhile, in a medium mixing bowl combine boiling water, couscous, and parsley. Cover; let stand for 5 minutes. Fluff with a fork before serving. Serve lamb kabobs with couscous. Makes 4 servings.

Nutrition Information Per Serving:
283 calories, 11 g total fat, 4 g saturated fat, 48 mg cholesterol, 42 mg sodium, 29 g carbohydrate, 5 g fiber, 16 g protein.

Use 1 teaspoon curry powder if you like curry and 2 teaspoons if you love it.

COOKING LEAN

Once you get your healthy cut of meat home from the store, there are a few more steps to take to make sure it gets to the table as lean as possible.

Even the leanest cuts of meat contain some separable fat that can be trimmed away with a sharp knife before cooking. This reduces the total fat and cholesterol in the cooked portion.

Cook it lean. The best cooking methods are broiling, grilling, pan-broiling, poaching, or roasting. Remember to roast and broil meats on a rack so fat drips away from the meat.

Forget about making gravy with the fatty drippings. If you want to serve a gravy with your meat, try one of the low-fat jars of gravy available at your grocery store.

Eliminate or reduce the amount of fat used to cook your meat. Use nonstick spray coating instead of oil to brown your meat and use low-fat or nonfat ingredients in the recipe.

For juicy results, cook lean meats to no more than medium doneness (160°). Lean meats cooked past this temperature tend to dry out and lose their flavor.

SPRING LAMB WITH ROSEMARY AND RHUBARB

A tangy rhubarb sauce perfectly complements the mild flavor of the lamb chops.

Nonstick spray coating
1½ **teaspoons snipped fresh rosemary** *or* ½ **teaspoon dried rosemary, crushed**
¼ **teaspoon seasoned salt**
8 **lamb loin chops, cut ¾-inch thick (about 1¼ pounds)**
¼ **teaspoon finely shredded orange peel**
⅓ **cup orange juice**
¼ **cup reduced-sodium chicken broth**
1 **tablespoon brown sugar**
2 **teaspoons cornstarch**
1 **cup chopped fresh rhubarb (about 2 to 3 medium stalks)** *or* **frozen unsweetened sliced rhubarb, chopped**
Orange peel strips (optional)
Rosemary sprigs (optional)

Spray the unheated rack of a broiler pan with nonstick spray coating. In a small bowl mix rosemary and seasoned salt; rub over lamb. Place lamb on rack. Broil 3 to 4 inches from the heat for 5 minutes. Turn lamb; broil for 4 to 6 minutes more for medium-rare or to desired doneness.

Meanwhile, for sauce, in a medium saucepan combine orange peel, orange juice, chicken broth, brown sugar, and cornstarch. Cook and stir till thickened and bubbly. Add rhubarb. Cover and simmer about 4 minutes for fresh rhubarb or 2 minutes for frozen rhubarb. Rhubarb should be tender.

To serve, spoon sauce over lamb chops. Garnish with orange peel strips and rosemary sprigs, if desired. Makes 4 servings.

Nutrition Information Per Serving: 222 calories, 9 g total fat, 3 g saturated fat, 80 mg cholesterol, 178 mg sodium, 8 g carbohydrate, 1 g fiber, 26 g protein.

MEDITERRANEAN LAMB CHOPS WITH TOMATOES

Serve this Mediterranean-inspired dish over hot cooked orzo, angel hair pasta, or thin vermicelli.

⅔ cup orzo *or* 4 ounces angel hair pasta
8 lamb rib chops, cut ¾-inch thick
½ teaspoon spicy salt-free seasoning *or* salt-free seasoning
1 cup reduced-sodium stewed tomatoes
1 clove garlic, minced
1 tablespoon lemon juice
½ teaspoon sugar
½ teaspoon dried thyme, crushed
¼ teaspoon dried oregano, crushed
¼ teaspoon finely shredded orange peel
¼ cup reduced-sodium chicken broth
2 teaspoons cornstarch

Prepare orzo or pasta according to package directions omitting margarine and salt. Meanwhile, season lamb with salt-free seasoning. Heat a large nonstick skillet over medium heat. Add lamb chops.

Cook lamb for 6 to 8 minutes or to desired doneness, turning once. Remove chops to platter; cover and keep warm.

Drain fat from skillet. In the same skillet combine stewed tomatoes, garlic, lemon juice, sugar, thyme, oregano, and orange peel. Bring to boiling. Combine broth with cornstarch. Stir into tomato mixture. Cook and stir till thickened and bubbly. Cook and stir for 2 minutes more. Serve the chops with the cooked orzo or pasta. Spoon sauce over all. Makes 4 servings.

Nutrition Information Per Serving: 353 calories, 12 g total fat, 4 g saturated fat, 77 mg cholesterol, 140 mg sodium, 32 g carbohydrate, 2 g fiber, 28 g protein.

MEATLESS MAIN DISHES

PINTO BEAN TACOS

8 taco shells
1 15-ounce can pinto beans,
     rinsed and drained
½ cup reduced-sodium tomato
     sauce
1 4-ounce can diced green chili
     peppers, drained
1 teaspoon chili powder
¼ teaspoon dried oregano,
     crushed
¼ teaspoon ground cumin
1½ cups shredded lettuce
1 medium tomato, chopped
½ cup shredded reduced-fat
     cheddar cheese (2 ounces)

Heat taco shells according to package directions.

Meanwhile, in a medium saucepan combine pinto beans, tomato sauce, chili peppers, chili powder, oregano, and cumin. Bring to boiling. Reduce heat; simmer, uncovered, for 5 minutes, stirring occasionally. Mash beans slightly, if desired.

Spoon bean mixture into taco shells. Pass lettuce, tomato, and cheese for toppings. Serve with salsa, if desired. Makes 4 servings.

Nutrition Information Per Serving:
276 calories, 8 g total fat, 2 g saturated fat, 10 mg cholesterol, 585 mg sodium, 40 g carbohydrate, 9 g fiber, 15 g protein.

Instead of tacos, create a batch of bean burritos. Spoon the bean mixture into four 10-inch flour tortillas. Sprinkle with lettuce, tomato, and cheese, and fold tortillas over filling.

SPICY STUFFED GREEN PEPPERS

Here's a recipe that gives you the chance to put your microwave to good use. Place the filled peppers on a microwave-safe plate and micro-cook on 100% power (high) for 2 to 3 minutes or till heated through.

4 large green peppers
1 15-ounce can black beans, rinsed and drained
1 8¾-ounce can whole kernel corn, drained
1 medium onion, chopped (½ cup)
⅓ cup long grain rice
1 to 2 jalapeño peppers, chopped
1 cup water
2 tablespoons snipped cilantro *or* ½ teaspoon ground coriander
¾ cup shredded reduced-fat Monterey Jack cheese (3 ounces)

Fill a large kettle half full of water; bring to boiling. Meanwhile, cut tops from green peppers; remove seeds. Chop tops; set aside. Add whole green peppers to boiling water; return to boiling. Reduce heat. Cover and cook for 4 to 5 minutes or till just tender.

Meanwhile, in a medium sauce-pan combine the chopped green pepper tops, black beans, corn, onion, rice, jalapeño peppers, and the 1 cup water. Bring to boiling. Reduce heat. Cover and simmer about 15 minutes or till rice is tender. Stir in cilantro or coriander and *half* of the cheese; toss to mix. If necessary, let filling stand, covered, about 5 minutes or till water is absorbed.

Fill peppers with rice mixture. Place in a 2-quart square baking dish; sprinkle with remaining cheese. Bake, uncovered, in a 400° oven about 5 minutes or till cheese melts. Makes 4 servings.

Nutrition Information Per Serving: 270 calories, 5 g total fat, 2 g saturated fat, 15 mg cholesterol, 510 mg sodium, 45 g carbohydrate, 8 g fiber, 16 g protein.

CHEESE SPIRALS WITH TOMATO SAUCE

½ **cup fat-free *or* light ricotta cheese**
½ **cup shredded part-skim mozzarella cheese**
2 **tablespoons grated Parmesan cheese**
1 **teaspoon dried basil, crushed**
½ **teaspoon dried marjoram, crushed**
1 **slightly beaten egg white**
8 **lasagna noodles, cooked and drained**
1 **14½-ounce can reduced-sodium stewed tomatoes**
½ **teaspoon dried basil, crushed**
¼ **teaspoon salt**
1 **tablespoon water**
1 **teaspoon cornstarch**

Mix ricotta cheese, mozzarella cheese, Parmesan cheese, 1 teaspoon basil, and marjoram. Add egg white; mix well. Spread about *2 tablespoons* cheese mixture on each noodle. Roll up from one end.

In a large skillet mix tomatoes, ½ teaspoon basil, and salt; bring to boiling. Mix water and cornstarch; add to tomato mixture. Cook and stir till bubbly. Place lasagna rolls, seam-side down, in skillet. Cover; simmer 12 to 15 minutes or till hot. Makes 4 servings.

Nutrition Information Per Serving:
278 calories, 4 g total fat, 2 g saturated fat, 13 mg cholesterol, 337 mg sodium, 45 g carbohydrate, 2 g fiber, 16 g protein.

This is like eating spirals of lasagna, but takes a lot less time and effort to make.

NATURAL AND PROCESS CHEESES

Cheese made directly from the curd of milk and not reprocessed or blended is known as natural cheese. Process cheese is made from natural cheese that has undergone additional steps, such as pasteurization. Process cheese often has other ingredients added to it for flavor, a softer texture, and longer shelf life.

To help hold the line on fat, look for lower-fat and nonfat natural and process cheeses. Here is an explanation of the cheeses commonly listed in the recipes for this book.

● Reduced-fat natural cheese: A natural cheese, such as cheddar, Swiss, and Monterey Jack cheese, with fewer grams of fat than regular natural cheese. Lower-fat mozzarella is called "part-skim mozzarella cheese."

● Lower-fat flavored process cheese product: A lower-fat process cheese that is available in American, cheddar, or Swiss flavors.

● Nonfat process cheese product: A process cheese without any fat.

VEGGIE-TOPPED COUSCOUS

If you're on the lookout for sodium, then rinse and drain the garbanzo beans to reduce some of their saltiness.

1 large onion, cut into thin wedges
2 cloves garlic, minced
1 teaspoon olive oil *or* cooking oil
2 cups thinly sliced carrots
½ cup water
1 teaspoon dried basil, crushed
½ teaspoon ground cumin
¼ teaspoon salt
⅛ teaspoon ground red pepper (optional)
2 medium zucchini, quartered lengthwise and cut into ½-inch pieces (2½ cups)
1 15-ounce can garbanzo beans, rinsed and drained
1 14½-ounce can reduced-sodium stewed tomatoes
2 tablespoons water
2 teaspoons cornstarch
2 cups reduced-sodium chicken broth
1 cup couscous
¼ cup chopped unsalted dry roasted peanuts

In a large saucepan cook onion and garlic in hot oil over medium-low heat till crisp-tender. Stir in carrots, ½ cup water, basil, cumin, salt, and, if desired, red pepper. Bring to boiling. Reduce heat. Cover and simmer for 10 minutes. Stir in zucchini, garbanzo beans, and tomatoes. Cover and cook for 2 minutes. Stir together 2 tablespoons water and cornstarch. Stir into tomato mixture. Cook and stir till thickened and bubbly. Cook and stir for 2 minutes more.

Meanwhile, in a medium saucepan bring chicken broth to boiling. Add couscous; cover and let stand for 5 minutes or till liquid is absorbed; fluff with fork. Serve vegetable mixture over hot couscous. Sprinkle with peanuts. Makes 4 servings.

Nutrition Information Per Serving: 451 calories, 8 g total fat, 1 g saturated fat, 0 mg cholesterol, 625 mg sodium, 81 g carbohydrate, 14 g fiber, 16 g protein.

VEGETABLE-MACARONI CASSEROLE

Try this healthy casserole instead of traditional macaroni and cheese. It's creamy and full of macaroni....just the way kids like it.

¾ **cup elbow macaroni**
1 **10-ounce package frozen mixed vegetables**
1 **medium zucchini, halved lengthwise and sliced**
1 **12-ounce can evaporated skim milk (1½ cups)**
½ **cup reduced-sodium chicken broth**
¼ **cup all-purpose flour**
½ **teaspoon dried oregano, crushed**
¼ **teaspoon garlic salt**
⅛ **teaspoon pepper**
 Nonstick spray coating
3 **tablespoons grated Parmesan cheese**
1 **medium tomato, sliced**
3 **tablespoons grated Parmesan cheese**

In a large saucepan cook macaroni according to package directions *except* omit salt and add mixed vegetables and zucchini the last 3 minutes of cooking. Drain. Return pasta mixture to saucepan.

Meanwhile, in a medium saucepan stir together milk, chicken broth, flour, oregano, garlic salt, and pepper. Cook and stir till thickened and bubbly. Add to drained pasta mixture; toss to coat. Spray a 2-quart square baking dish with nonstick spray coating. Spoon macaroni mixture into dish.

Bake in a 375° oven for 10 minutes. Top with sliced tomato and sprinkle with Parmesan cheese. Bake about 5 minutes more or till heated through. Let stand for 5 minutes before serving. Makes 4 servings.

Nutrition Information Per Serving: 261 calories, 2 g total fat, 1 g saturated fat, 8 mg cholesterol, 404 mg sodium, 45 g carbohydrate, 1 g fiber, 15 g protein.

CHEESE POLENTA WITH PASTA SAUCE

1 cup yellow cornmeal
  Dash bottled hot pepper
  sauce
1 cup shredded part-skim *or*
  nonfat mozzarella cheese
¼ cup grated Parmesan cheese
⅔ cup chopped green pepper
1 cup reduced-sodium,
  reduced-fat meatless
  spaghetti sauce

In large saucepan bring 2¾ cups *water* to boiling. Combine cornmeal, hot pepper sauce, and 1 cup *cold water*. Slowly add cornmeal mixture to boiling water, stirring constantly. Cook and stir till mixture returns to boiling. Reduce heat; cook for 10 to 15 minutes or till very thick, stirring often.

Pour *half* of the mixture into a 9-inch pie plate; spread evenly. Sprinkle with mozzarella cheese and *2 tablespoons* of the Parmesan cheese. Top with peppers. Spread remaining cornmeal mixture evenly on top. (If mixture becomes too thick, add a little additional water.) Sprinkle with remaining Parmesan cheese. Cover and refrigerate for several hours or overnight till firm.

Bake, uncovered, in a 400° oven for 30 to 35 minutes or till golden and heated through.

Meanwhile, heat spaghetti sauce. To serve, cut polenta into four wedges; top with sauce. Makes 4 servings.

Nutrition Information Per Serving:
257 calories, 7 g total fat, 4 g saturated fat, 21 mg cholesterol, 435 mg sodium, 33 g carbohydrate, 2 g fiber, 14 g protein.

This meatless Italian one-dish meal is made in advance and refrigerated for up to 24 hours. This allows the cornmeal mixture to firm up so you can cut it into wedges after it's baked.

MAKE AHEAD

MEATLESS MATCHMAKING

Today's vegetarians have a wide variety of foods to choose from to adhere to a meatless diet. But it's a matter of matchmaking the right legumes, grains, and vegetables to meet proper nutritional goals.

Plant proteins are not as high in quality as animal proteins. That's why it's important to combine them so they mimic the high quality proteins found in meat. Some of the complementary proteins are listed below as a guide. Simply combine any legume with any grain, nut, or seed. Keep in mind that combining any of the legumes, grains, or nuts or seeds with egg or milk products will also make a high-quality protein.

Legumes	Grains	Nuts or Seeds
lentils	rice	cashews
dried beans	wheat	pecans
split peas	corn	sunflower seeds
tofu	barley	sesame seeds
peanuts	oats	almonds

VEGETABLE CABBAGE ROLLS WITH BULGUR

¾ cup reduced-sodium chicken
   or beef broth
1 small green sweet pepper,
   chopped (½ cup)
1 small red sweet pepper,
   chopped (½ cup)
1 small zucchini, quartered
   lengthwise and sliced
   (1 cup)
1½ cups chopped fresh
   mushrooms (4 ounces)
½ cup bulgur
1 teaspoon dried basil, crushed
½ teaspoon dried marjoram,
   crushed
½ teaspoon dried thyme,
   crushed
¼ teaspoon pepper
8 medium cabbage leaves
¼ cup finely shredded *or* grated
   Parmesan cheese
2 teaspoons lemon *or* lime juice
1 8-ounce can reduced-sodium
   tomato sauce
⅛ to ¼ teaspoon bottled hot
   pepper sauce
2 tablespoons finely shredded
   or grated Parmesan cheese

In a large saucepan combine broth, red pepper, green pepper, zucchini, mushrooms, bulgur, basil, marjoram, thyme, and pepper. Bring to boiling. Reduce heat. Cover and simmer for 5 minutes. Remove from heat; let stand, covered, for 5 minutes.

Meanwhile, fill a large kettle or Dutch oven with water; bring to boiling. Remove center vein from cabbage leaves, keeping each leaf in one piece. Immerse leaves, *four* at a time, into the boiling water for 2 to 3 minutes or till leaves are limp. Drain well.

Stir ¼ cup Parmesan cheese and lemon or lime juice into bulgur mixture. Place about ¼ *cup* of the bulgur mixture on each cabbage leaf. Fold in sides, starting at an unfolded edge, carefully roll up each leaf enclosing filling. Stir hot pepper sauce into tomato sauce. Spoon about ⅓ *cup* of the tomato sauce into a 2-quart square baking dish. Place cabbage rolls in dish. Spoon remaining sauce over cabbage rolls. Cover dish with foil. Bake in a 400° oven about 15 minutes or till heated through. Sprinkle with 2 tablespoons Parmesan cheese before serving. Makes 4 servings.

Nutrition Information Per Serving:
160 calories, 3 g total fat, 2 g saturated fat, 7 mg cholesterol, 282 mg sodium, 26 g carbohydrate, 8 g fiber, 9 g protein.

Bulgur is made from parched cracked wheat and gives these cabbage rolls a delicate nutty flavor. It's a good choice for busy schedules because bulgur is precooked when you buy it so it cooks quickly or needs only a brief soaking before using.

CHILI-SAUCED PASTA

6 ounces refrigerated linguine
**1 14½ -ounce can reduced-
    sodium stewed tomatoes**
**1 medium green pepper, cut
    into thin strips, about
    2-inches long**
**2 tablespoons reduced-sodium
    tomato paste**
3 teaspoons chili powder
¼ teaspoon salt
¼ teaspoon garlic powder
¼ teaspoon ground cumin
**1 8-ounce can kidney beans,
    rinsed and drained**
¼ cup water
2 teaspoons cornstarch

Cook pasta according to package directions except omit salt; drain. Set aside and keep warm.

Meanwhile, in a medium saucepan combine tomatoes, green pepper strips, tomato paste, chili powder, salt, garlic powder, and cumin. Bring to boiling. Reduce heat. Cover and simmer for 3 minutes. Stir in kidney beans.

Stir together water and cornstarch; add to tomato mixture. Cook and stir till thickened and bubbly. Cook and stir for 2 minutes more. Serve tomato mixture over hot pasta. Makes 3 servings.

Nutrition Information Per Serving:
322 calories, 2 g total fat, 0 g saturated fat, 49 mg cholesterol, 392 mg sodium, 65 g carbohydrate, 10 g fiber, 15 g protein.

You can use dried pasta instead of fresh in this 15 minute recipe, but plan on adding a few more minutes to the cooking time.

TOFU AND BROCCOLI STIR-FRY

For stir-fries like this one, opt for firm-style tofu which holds its shape better than soft-style. And, stir it gently so it doesn't break up.

⅔ cup water
2 tablespoons dry sherry
2 tablespoons reduced-sodium soy sauce
4 teaspoons cornstarch
¼ teaspoon ground ginger
¼ teaspoon crushed red pepper
   Nonstick spray coating
2 cloves garlic, minced
3 cups broccoli cut into bite-size pieces
½ cup sliced carrot
1 medium onion, cut into wedges
1 cup fresh bean sprouts
1 pound tofu (bean curd), cut into ½-inch cubes
2 cups hot cooked rice

In a small mixing bowl stir together the water, sherry, soy sauce, cornstarch, ginger, and crushed red pepper; set aside.

Spray a cold wok or large skillet with nonstick coating. Preheat wok or large skillet over medium heat. Add the garlic; stir-fry for 15 seconds. Add the broccoli and carrot; stir-fry for 3 minutes. Add the onion; stir-fry for 3 minutes. Add the bean sprouts; stir-fry for 1 minute. Push the vegetables from the center of the wok or skillet.

Stir soy sauce mixture; add to the center of the wok. Cook and stir till thickened and bubbly. Cook and stir for 2 minutes more. Stir the vegetables into sauce. Stir in tofu. Heat through. Serve with hot cooked rice. Makes 4 servings.

Nutrition Information Per Serving: 355 calories, 12 g total fat, 2 g saturated fat, 0 mg cholesterol, 334 mg sodium, 42 g carbohydrate, 8 g fiber, 25 g protein.

CABBAGE-PASTA BAKE

4 ounces spinach *or* plain
    fettuccine
1 cup thinly sliced carrots
½ of a 16-ounce package
    (4 cups) coleslaw mix
    (shredded cabbage with
    carrot)
1 cup reduced-sodium chicken
    broth
1 teaspoon caraway seed
¼ teaspoon pepper
⅛ teaspoon salt
1 12-ounce carton low-fat
    cottage cheese
1 tablespoon horseradish
    mustard
½ cup skim milk
1 tablespoon cornstarch
1 tablespoon snipped chives
    Nonstick spray coating
½ cup crispy rye cracker
    crumbs

Prepare fettuccine according to package directions except omit the salt and add sliced carrots the last 5 minutes of cooking. Drain well; set aside.

Meanwhile, in a large saucepan combine coleslaw mix, chicken broth, caraway seed, pepper, and salt. Bring to boiling. Reduce heat. Cover and simmer for 5 minutes. Stir in undrained cottage cheese and mustard. Stir together milk and cornstarch. Add to hot mixture. Cook and stir till thickened and bubbly. Cook and stir for 2 minutes more. Stir in chives and drained pasta mixture; toss to mix.

Spray a 2-quart square baking dish with nonstick spray coating. Turn pasta mixture into dish. Sprinkle with cracker crumbs. Bake in a 375° oven for 15 to 20 minutes or till heated through and bubbly. Makes 4 to 6 servings.

Nutrition Information Per Serving:
245 calories, 2 g total fat, 1 g saturated fat, 4 mg cholesterol, 663 mg sodium, 39 g carbohydrate, 4 g fiber, 18 g protein.

Take your pick: use fresh refrigerated fettuccine or dried fettuccine in this German-flavored meatless main dish.

PEPPERS WITH COUSCOUS-CHICKPEA PILAF

You'll find couscous instead of rice stuffed inside these sweet peppers. Couscous, a ground semolina grain in the shape of very small beads, can be found in the rice or pasta section of your supermarket or at specialty stores.

4 medium green *or* red sweet
   peppers
1¼ cup reduced-sodium chicken
   broth
1 15-ounce can garbanzo
   beans, rinsed and drained
¼ cup chopped onion
1 large clove garlic, minced
1 teaspoon ground cumin
1 teaspoon toasted sesame oil
1 cup couscous
1 cup reduced-sodium,
   reduced-fat meatless
   spaghetti sauce

Fill a large saucepan half full of water. Bring to boiling.

Meanwhile, cut about 1-inch off the top of each pepper. Discard seeds and membranes. Finely chop the pepper tops (you should have about ¾ cup). Add pepper shells to boiling water; cook for 5 minutes. Drain on paper towels. (If desired, peppers can be micro-cooked. Place peppers, cut side down in a 2-quart square microwave-safe baking dish. Cover dish with microwave-safe plastic wrap. Cook on 100% power (high) for 5 to 7 minutes or till crisp-tender, turning dish once.)

In a medium saucepan combine chicken broth, garbanzo beans, onion, garlic, cumin, sesame oil, and chopped pepper. Bring to boiling; reduce heat. Simmer for 2 minutes. Stir in couscous. Remove from heat; cover and let stand for 5 minutes.

Place drained peppers in a 2-quart square baking dish. Fluff couscous mixture with a fork. Fill peppers with couscous mixture. Spoon any remaining couscous mixture into the dish around the peppers. Bake in a 375° oven about 15 minutes or till heated through.(Or, cover with vented plastic wrap. Micro-cook on high for 2 to 3 minutes or till heated through, turning dish once.

Meanwhile, in a small saucepan heat the spaghetti sauce. To serve, spoon sauce over stuffed peppers. Makes 4 servings.

Nutrition Information Per Serving:
364 calories, 3 g total fat, 0 g saturated fat, 0 mg cholesterol, 536 mg sodium, 70 g carbohydrate, 10 g fiber, 13 g protein.

MUSHROOM-BARLEY CHOWDER

Be sure to buy quick-cooking barley which cooks in 10 minutes instead of pearl barley which takes about 40 minutes to cook.

3 cups sliced fresh mushrooms (8 ounces)
1 14½-ounce can reduced-sodium chicken broth
8 green onions, sliced (½ cup)
½ cup quick-cooking barley
½ teaspoon dried basil, crushed
⅛ teaspoon pepper
1 16½-ounce can reduced-sodium cream-style corn
1 12-ounce can evaporated skim milk

In a large saucepan combine mushrooms, broth, green onion, barley, basil, and pepper. Bring to boiling. Reduce heat; cover and simmer about 10 minutes or till barley is tender. Stir in corn and milk. Cook and stir till heated through. Makes 4 servings.

Nutrition Information Per Serving: 362 calories, 2 g total fat, 0 g saturated fat, 4 mg cholesterol, 302 mg sodium, 75 g carbohydrate, 3 g fiber, 16 g protein.

TOFU TIDBITS

Tofu is a funny-sounding food with a plain-looking appearance and a relatively bland taste. But don't let that fool you because it's packed with a wallop of good nutrition that meatless eaters can capitalize on. A ½ cup portion of regular tofu contains about 95 calories, 10 grams of protein, 6 grams of fat (all unsaturated), and no cholesterol.

Thanks to its growing popularity, there are more kinds of tofu on the market to choose from. Silken tofu is a Japanese style of tofu with the softest texture of all. Chinese tofu is firmer than silken tofu but is still smooth and creamy. Regular Chinese or Japanese tofu is pressed longer than silken or Chinese tofu to remove more water, giving it a firmer texture. Firm and extra-firm tofu contain less water than other types of tofu and have a somewhat grainy texture. Soft tofu is good for sauces and simmered recipes. Firm tofu is good in casseroles and stir-fry recipes where you want the tofu to remain intact.

Fresh tofu should be covered with water and refrigerated in an airtight container and stored for up to 1 week. Change the water daily to keep the tofu fresh and moist. You can also freeze tofu up to 3 months but the texture may become less tender and smooth. For shelf-stable tofu, follow label directions for storage information.

MOUTH-WATERING SIDES

Fruited Spinach Salad with Currant Vinaigrette

FRUITED SPINACH SALAD WITH CURRANT VINAIGRETTE

¼ **cup currant jelly**
3 **tablespoons red wine vinegar**
8 **cups cleaned spinach leaves, stems removed**
1 **cup fresh strawberries, halved**
1 **11-ounce can mandarin orange sections, drained**
4 **green onions, sliced (¼ cup)**

For the vinaigrette, in a small saucepan combine currant jelly and vinegar. Cook and stir over medium-low heat just till jelly melts and mixture is smooth. Chill in the freezer for 10 minutes.

Meanwhile, in a large salad bowl combine spinach, strawberries, orange sections, and green onion. Drizzle vinaigrette over the spinach mixture; toss to mix. Serve immediately. Makes 6 servings.

Nutrition Information Per Serving:
46 calories, 0 g total fat, 0 g saturated fat, 0 mg cholesterol, 72 mg sodium, 11 g carbohydrate, 3 g fiber, 2 g protein.

Currant jelly and red wine vinegar team up for a speedy, two-ingredient dressing.

ORANGE AND BEET SALAD

6 **cups torn cleaned spinach, leaf lettuce, *and/or* romaine**
1 **8-ounce can beets, drained and cut into julienne strips**
3 **oranges, peeled and thinly sliced**
½ **of a medium cucumber, thinly sliced**
½ **cup nonfat Italian salad dressing**

Divide greens among six salad plates. Top each serving with some of the beets, orange slices, and cucumber slices. Serve with dressing. Makes 6 servings.

Nutrition Information Per Serving:
42 calories, 0 g total fat, 0 g saturated fat, 0 mg cholesterol, 383 mg sodium, 9 g carbohydrate, 3 g fiber, 2 g protein.

Chill the canned beets overnight in the refrigerator, so they will be refreshingly cold when it's time to make the salad.

ITALIAN RICE AND ARTICHOKE SALAD

The dried tomatoes may still be a little chewy after soaking, but they will soften up in the salad as it chills.

MAKE AHEAD

1⅓ cups water
1 9-ounce package frozen
    artichoke hearts
¼ teaspoon salt
⅔ cup long grain rice
3 dried tomatoes
2 tablespoons olive oil *or*
    salad oil
2 tablespoons lemon juice
¼ teaspoon garlic powder *or*
    1 garlic clove, minced
¼ teaspoon pepper
4 green onions, sliced (¼ cup)
1 tablespoon snipped fresh
    basil *or* ½ teaspoon dried
    basil, crushed
2 tablespoons grated Parmesan
    cheese

In a medium saucepan, place the water, artichoke hearts, and salt. Bring to boiling. Stir in the rice. Cover and simmer for 15 to 20 minutes or till rice is tender.

Meanwhile, in a small bowl soak tomatoes in enough cold water to cover for 15 minutes.

For dressing, in a screw-top jar combine oil, lemon juice, garlic, and pepper. Cover and shake well. Set aside.

Drain and snip tomatoes. In a large bowl combine rice mixture, green onion, Parmesan cheese, basil, and snipped tomatoes. Shake dressing again; pour over the rice mixture. Toss to coat. Cover and chill for 2 to 24 hours. Makes 4 to 6 servings.

Nutrition Information Per Serving:
229 calories, 9 g total fat, 2 g saturated fat, 2 mg cholesterol, 294 mg sodium, 33 g carbohydrate, 5 g fiber, 6 g protein.

TANGY CUKES AND MUSHROOMS

1 **medium cucumber, thinly sliced (1⅓ cups)**
3 **cups sliced fresh mushrooms (8 ounces)**
1 **small red *or* green sweet pepper, cut in strips**
4 **green onions, sliced (¼ cup)**
½ **cup white wine vinegar**
¼ **cup sugar**
1 **tablespoon snipped fresh dill or ¾ teaspoon dried dillweed**
¼ **teaspoon salt**
⅛ **teaspoon pepper**

In a large bowl combine cucumber slices, mushrooms, pepper strips, and green onion.

In a small bowl combine vinegar, sugar, dill, salt, and pepper. Stir till the sugar is dissolved. Pour over the cucumber mixture; toss to coat. Cover and chill for 2 to 24 hours, stirring occasionally. Serve with a slotted spoon. Makes 4 to 6 servings.

Nutrition Information Per Serving: 52 calories, 1 g total fat, 0 g saturated fat, 0 mg cholesterol, 72 mg sodium, 11 g carbohydrate, 1 g fiber, 3 g protein.

If you have some leftover cooked small pasta (about 1/2 cup), stir it into this crisp and creamy salad.

MAKE AHEAD

SALAD DRESSING SMARTS

You'll find a dizzying array of salad dressings and mayonnaise on the supermarket shelves. Right beside the regular dressings and mayonnaise are a vast selection of reduced-calorie, low-calorie, nonfat, and no-cholesterol products. To sort through it all, simply become a label reader and look at the nutrition information on each product. In a glance you can compare calories, fat, cholesterol, and sodium and then choose the one that best fits your needs.

ASPARAGUS AND FENNEL SALAD

If you opt for the Herbed Oil-Free Dressing, mix it up the night before.

1 medium fennel bulb
3 cups torn Boston *or* bibb lettuce
1⅓ cups fresh asparagus cut into 1-inch pieces
1 cup sliced fresh mushrooms
⅓ cup Herbed Oil-Free Dressing *or* bottled nonfat clear salad dressing

Clean fennel. Trim off leaves; chop ¼ cup leaves and set aside. Discard stalks and core. Cut fennel bulb into thin strips.

In large bowl combine fennel strips, reserved fennel leaves, lettuce, asparagus, and mushrooms. (If desired, cover and chill lettuce mixture till serving time.)

To serve, drizzle dressing over salad mixture; toss to coat. Serve immediately. Makes 4 servings.

Herbed Oil-Free Dressing: In a small mixing bowl stir together 1 tablespoon *powdered fruit pectin;* ¾ teaspoon snipped fresh or ¼ teaspoon dried *oregano, basil, thyme,* or *savory,* crushed; ½ teaspoon *sugar;* ⅛ teaspoon *dry mustard;* and ⅛ teaspoon *pepper.* Add ¼ cup *water;* 1 tablespoon *vinegar;* and 1 small clove *garlic,* minced. Beat till mixed. Cover and store in the refrigerator at least 1 hour or up to 3 days. Makes about ⅓ cup.

Nutrition Information Per Serving:
39 calories, 1 g total fat, 0 g saturated fat, 0 mg cholesterol, 24 mg sodium, 7 g carbohydrate, 1 g fiber, 3 g protein.

SHREDDED ZUCCHINI AND CARROT SALAD

Your food processor can make easy work of this pretty shredded salad. If you shred the vegetables by hand, add about 10 more minutes to the preparation time.

2 **medium zucchini**
1 **medium carrot**
1 **onion wedge**
   (¼ **small onion**)
⅓ **cup raisins**
⅓ **cup plain nonfat yogurt**
¼ **cup unsalted dry roasted**
   peanuts
2 **teaspoons snipped fresh dill**
   or ½ **teaspoon dried**
   dillweed
⅛ **teaspoon pepper**
4 **lettuce leaves**

Using a food processor, coarsely shred zucchini, carrot, and onion wedge. Drain any excess liquid.

Combine shredded vegetables, raisins, yogurt, peanuts, dill, and pepper. Mix well. Serve on lettuce leaves. Makes 4 servings.

Nutrition Information Per Serving:
145 calories, 5 g total fat, 1 g saturated fat, 1 mg cholesterol, 59 mg sodium, 21 g carbohydrate, 3 g fiber, 7 g protein.

HOT ORIENTAL COLESLAW

If the frozen pea pods stick together, run them under cold water to thaw slightly.

¼ **cup water**
2 **tablespoons reduced-sodium**
   soy sauce
1 **teaspoon cornstarch**
⅛ **teaspoon ground ginger**
⅛ **teaspoon crushed red**
   pepper
4 **cups coleslaw mix (shredded**
   cabbage with carrot)
1 **6-ounce package frozen pea**
   pods, halved crosswise
4 **green onions, sliced (¼ cup)**

In a medium saucepan stir together water, soy sauce, cornstarch, ginger, and crushed red pepper. Cook and stir over medium heat till thickened and bubbly. Add the coleslaw mix, frozen pea pods, and green onions. Cook and stir just till cabbage is wilted and pea pods are tender. Makes 4 servings.

Nutrition Information Per Serving:
61 calories, 0 g total fat, 0 g saturated fat, 0 mg cholesterol, 298 mg sodium, 13 g carbohydrate, 6 g fiber, 3 g protein.

FRESH BASIL, TOMATO, AND ONION SALAD

4 lettuce leaves
4 small ripe tomatoes, cored and thinly sliced
2 slices sweet red onion, separated into rings
2 tablespoons snipped fresh basil
¼ cup nonfat Italian salad dressing
   Fresh basil (optional)

Line four salad plates with lettuce. Arrange tomato slices and onion rings on lettuce. Sprinkle with chopped basil; drizzle with dressing. Garnish with additional fresh basil, if desired. Makes 4 servings.

Nutrition Information Per Serving:
29 calories, 0 g total fat, 0 g saturated fat, 0 mg cholesterol, 220 mg sodium, 6 g carbohydrate, 1 g fiber, 1 g protein.

Make this salad when tomatoes are at their best, during the hot days of summer.

PAMPER YOUR GREENS

In order for salad greens to be their freshest when you bring that salad to the table, follow a few easy steps once you get them home from the store.

● To clean leafy greens: Remove and discard any outer leaves that are bruised, discolored, tough, or wilted. Wash the remaining leaves under cold water. Drain thoroughly and place on paper towels or a clean kitchen towel. Place a second towel over them and gently pat dry. Or, dry them in a salad spinner.

● To clean iceberg lettuce: Remove and discard any outer leaves that are bruised, discolored, tough, or wilted. Remove the core by hitting the stem end sharply on a countertop. Then twist the core and lift it out. Place the head of lettuce, core side up, under cold running water to rinse the leaves. Invert the head and let drain thoroughly.

●To store greens: Place the clean and dry greens in a plastic bag or airtight container and store in them in the refrigerator. They should stay crisp and fresh for three or four days.

● To crisp greens that are limp: Wash greens and place them in a plastic bag while they're still slightly damp. Refrigerate for at least 8 hours.

Tossed Greens and Jicama

TOSSED GREENS AND JICAMA

½ of a 10-ounce package
    ready-to-use mixed salad
    greens (4 cups)
1 cup sliced fresh mushrooms
1 cup jicama strips
½ cup sliced water chestnuts
½ medium red sweet pepper,
    cut in bite-size pieces
⅓ cup nonfat Italian salad
    dressing
2 tablespoons reduced-sodium
    soy sauce
1 tablespoon dry sherry

In a large bowl combine greens, mushrooms, jicama, water chestnuts, and red sweet pepper. For dressing, in a screw-top jar combine Italian dressing, soy sauce, and sherry. Cover and shake well. Drizzle dressing over salad; toss to coat. Makes 4 servings.

Nutrition Information Per Serving:
68 calories, 1 g total fat, 0 g saturated fat, 0 mg cholesterol, 563 mg sodium, 13 g carbohydrate, 1 g fiber, 3 g protein.

If you're fresh out of jicama, use bean sprouts instead.

CHUTNEY-PINEAPPLE SLAW

2 tablespoons snipped chutney
½ teaspoon finely shredded
    orange peel
2 tablespoons orange juice
3 cups coleslaw mix (shredded
    cabbage with carrot)
1 8-ounce can pineapple
    tidbits, (juice pack)
    drained
¼ cup light *or* dark raisins

In a large bowl combine chutney, orange peel, and orange juice. Stir to mix well. Add coleslaw mix, pineapple tidbits, and raisins; toss to mix. Serve immediately or cover and chill till serving time. Makes 4 to 6 servings.

Nutrition Information Per Serving:
95 calories, 0 g total fat, 0 g saturated fat, 0 mg cholesterol, 16 mg sodium, 24 g carbohydrate, 2 g fiber, 1 g protein.

Chutney is an East Indian fruit or vegetable relish that can be smooth or chunky and sweet or tart. Sometimes it's even spicy-hot. Choose whichever type suits your taste.

WILTED SPINACH WITH RASPBERRY VINAIGRETTE

Packaged cleaned spinach is a timesaver, but supermarket salad bar spinach is even quicker. Save yourself a few preparation minutes and buy 10 to 12 cups of torn salad bar spinach instead of packaged spinach.

1 10-ounce package
    cleaned spinach
2 teaspoons olive oil *or* salad oil
3 cloves garlic, minced
2 tablespoons raspberry jelly
    or seedless raspberry
    preserves
2 tablespoons red wine vinegar
¼ teaspoon salt
    Dash pepper

Tear spinach, discarding stems (you should have 10 to 12 cups).

In a 12-inch skillet heat oil. Stir-fry garlic over medium-high heat for 30 seconds. Add raspberry jelly, vinegar, salt, and pepper. Heat and stir till the jelly melts and mixture boils. Remove the skillet from the heat. Add spinach. Toss till coated and spinach begins to wilt. Serve immediately. Makes 4 servings.

Nutrition Information Per Serving:
66 calories, 3 g total fat, 0 g saturated fat, 0 mg cholesterol, 191 mg sodium, 11 g carbohydrate, 2 g fiber, 2 g protein.

COTTAGE CHEESE-AND-MORE SALAD

The "more" comes from yellow or green sweet peppers, crushed pineapple, shredded carrot, and nonfat mayonnaise dressing.

1 medium yellow *or* green
    sweet pepper
2 cups low-fat cottage cheese,
    drained
1 8-ounce can crushed
    pineapple (juice pack),
    drained
½ cup shredded carrot
¼ cup nonfat mayonnaise
    dressing *or* salad dressing
6 lettuce leaves

Chop half of the yellow or green pepper. Cut the remaining half into thin strips; set aside.

In a medium bowl combine cottage cheese, pineapple, carrot, and chopped pepper. Add mayonnaise or salad dressing; stir to mix well. Cover and chill till serving time. Serve immediately or cover and chill. Serve on lettuce leaves. Garnish with the pepper strips. Makes 6 servings.

Nutrition Information Per Serving:
98 calories, 1 g total fat, 0 g saturated fat, 3 mg cholesterol, 438 mg sodium, 13 g carbohydrate, 1 g fiber, 10 g protein.

CREAMY CHILLED FRUIT SOUP

2　8-ounce cartons vanilla
　　low-fat yogurt
2　cups frozen unsweetened
　　peach slices
1　cup frozen unsweetened
　　whole strawberries
　　Dash nutmeg
⅓　cup orange juice
　　Sliced fresh strawberries
　　(optional)

In a blender container or food processor bowl combine *one* carton of yogurt, peaches, strawberries, and nutmeg. Cover and blend or process till smooth. Pour mixture into a bowl. Stir in remaining yogurt and orange juice. Mix well. Garnish with sliced strawberries, if desired. Makes 4 servings.

Nutrition Information Per Serving:
179 calories, 2 g total fat, 1 g saturated fat, 7 mg cholesterol, 81 mg sodium, 34 g carbohydrate, 2 g fiber, 7 g protein.

Serve this refreshing soup as a side dish with a sandwich or try it as a unique dessert.

A VARIETY OF VINEGARS

Gone are the days when distilled and cider were your only vinegar choices. Here's a rundown of old and new vinegar varieties for splashing in your next recipe.

Cider vinegar is derived from fermented apples and has a slightly fruity flavor and tawny color. It's a good choice when a recipe calls for "vinegar." Use it for pickles, chutneys, relishes, and salad dressings when its darker color won't affect your recipe.

Distilled vinegar, also called white vinegar, is made from grains such as corn, rye, and barley. Its somewhat harsh flavor lends itself best to pickling.

Malt vinegar is made from ale and fermented potatoes or grain, giving it a brownish color and yeasty flavor. It's best known for splashing on English fish and chips but can be used in recipes calling for cider vinegar.

Wine vinegars are made from wine, sherry, or champagne and are the mildest and most versatile of all the vinegars. Use them in salad dressings or sprinkled over fish.

Rice wine vinegar starts with sake (Japanese rice wine) and has a clean, mild taste. The slightly sweet taste complements salads as well as Japanese rice dishes.

Fruit and herb vinegars are made from either cider, distilled, or wine vinegars and flavored with the natural flavors of fruits or herbs. Try them in marinades or salad dressings.

Balsamic vinegar is made from the unfermented juice of high sugar grapes and aged in wooden barrels. The finished vinegar must be at least 6 years old, resulting in an intense, dark brown vinegar that is both sour and sweet. It makes an outstanding vinegar for salad dressing.

Creamy Spinach Soup

CREAMY SPINACH SOUP

1 10½-ounce can reduced-fat,
    reduced-sodium condensed
    cream of chicken soup
2 green onions, sliced
    (2 tablespoons)
    Dash ground nutmeg
    Dash pepper
4 cups cleaned spinach leaves,
    stems removed
1 12-ounce can evaporated
    skim milk
    Carrot cut-outs (optional)

In a blender container or food processor bowl combine soup, green onion, nutmeg, and pepper. Add spinach leaves, a few at a time, while blending or processing till mixture is nearly smooth. Pour into a medium saucepan. Stir in evaporated milk. Bring to boiling. Reduce heat; simmer, uncovered, for 2 minutes, stirring occasionally. Serve soup in bowls and garnish with carrot cut-outs, if desired. Makes 4 servings.

Nutrition Information Per Serving:
114 calories, 1 g total fat, 0 g saturated fat, 7 mg cholesterol, 316 mg sodium, 17 g carbohydrate, 2 g fiber, 10 g protein.

Use tiny cutters and thin slices of carrots to make the carrot cut-outs.

SQUASH SOUP

1 12-ounce package frozen
    mashed winter squash
1 cup reduced-sodium chicken
    broth
1 tablespoon fresh *or*
    freeze-dried snipped chives
1 teaspoon snipped fresh thyme
    or ¼ teaspon dried thyme,
    crushed
¼ teaspoon pepper
½ cup pear *or* apricot nectar
    Plain lowfat yogurt
    (optional)
    Ground nutmeg (optional)

In a medium saucepan, combine frozen squash, chicken broth, chives, thyme, and pepper. Bring to boiling. Reduce heat; cover and simmer for 8 to 10 minutes or till smooth, stirring occasionally. Stir in the nectar. Heat through.

Serve in soup bowls. If desired, dollop with yogurt and sprinkle with nutmeg. Makes 4 servings.

Nutrition Information Per Serving:
73 calories, 1 g total fat, 0 g saturated fat, 0 mg cholesterol, 54 mg sodium, 18 g carbohydrate, 3 g fiber, 1 g protein.

Serve this velvety smooth, slightly sweet soup as an opener to a chicken, turkey, or pork dinner.

ROMAINE AND PEA SOUP

Romaine is just as at home in this soup as it is in a salad. Choose romaine that is fresh looking and heavy and avoid leaves that are shriveled or brown.

2 cups reduced-sodium chicken broth
6 cups chopped romaine, ribs removed
1 cup frozen peas
4 green onions, chopped (¼ cup)
½ teaspoon fines herbes *or* ¼ teaspoon dried thyme, crushed
1 clove garlic, minced
1 tablespoon cornstarch
½ cup plain nonfat yogurt
Plain nonfat yogurt (optional)

In a medium saucepan combine *½ cup* of the chicken broth, romaine, peas, green onion, fines herbes or thyme, and garlic. Bring to boiling. Reduce heat; simmer, covered, for 6 to 8 minutes or till peas are very tender. Transfer mixture to a blender container or food processor bowl. Cover and blend or process till smooth. Add cornstarch and ½ cup yogurt. Blend or process till mixed. Return to saucepan. Stir in remaining broth. Cook and stir till thickened and bubbly. Cook and stir for 2 minutes more. If desired, dollop individual servings with additional yogurt. Makes 4 to 6 servings.

Nutrition Information Per Serving:
78 calories, 0 g total fat, 0 g saturated fat, 1 mg cholesterol, 268 mg sodium, 13 g carbohydrate, 3 g fiber, 6 g protein.

SOUR CREAM STAND-INS

There's no need to add the fat and calories of regular sour cream to recipes when you have these nifty substitutes. Take a look at them below and compare the amount of calories, fat, and cholesterol for 8 ounces before making your choice.

	Calories	Fat	Cholesterol
Dairy sour cream	486	48 g	101 mg
Light dairy sour cream	293	15 g	29 mg
Fat-free dairy sour cream	240	0 g	0 mg
Plain low-fat yogurt	144	4 g	14 mg
Plain nonfat yogurt	127	0 g	4 mg

TOMATO FENNEL BISQUE

1 pound plum tomatoes, quartered
1 14 ½-ounce can reduced-sodium chicken broth
1 large fennel bulb, coarsely chopped (about 2 cups)
1 large onion, coarsely chopped (1 cup)
1 clove garlic, minced
½ teaspoon savory, crushed
⅛ teaspoon pepper
Snipped parsley *or* chives (optional)

In a large saucepan combine tomatoes, chicken broth, fennel, onion, garlic, savory, and pepper. Bring to boiling. Reduce heat; cover and simmer for 10 to 15 minutes or till vegetables are tender. In a blender container or food processor bowl, blend or process *half* of the mixture, till nearly smooth. Strain to remove tomato seeds and skins. Return to saucepan. Repeat with remaining mixture. Heat through. Garnish with parsley or chives, if desired. Makes 4 servings.

Nutrition Information Per Serving:
70 calories, 1 g total fat, 0 g saturated fat, 0 mg cholesterol, 218 mg sodium, 15 g carbohydrate, 1 g fiber, 3 g protein.

Try this mild fennel-flavored soup as a first course to a special dinner.

BORSCHT

1 16-ounce can diced beets
1 14 ½-ounce can reduced-sodium tomatoes, cut up
1 14 ½-ounce can reduced-sodium chicken broth
2 cups coleslaw mix (shredded cabbage with carrot)
1 teaspoon sugar
½ teaspoon dried dillweed
¼ teaspoon celery seed
½ cup light dairy sour cream
2 green onions, sliced (2 tablespoons)

In a large saucepan combine *undrained* beets, *undrained* tomatoes, broth, coleslaw mix, sugar, dillweed, and celery seed. Bring to boiling; reduce heat. Cover and simmer for 10 to 15 minutes or till vegetables are very tender. (For a smoother soup, mash or puree half of the mixture.) Serve in soup bowls. Dollop with sour cream and sprinkle with green onion. Makes 6 servings.

Nutrition Information Per Serving:
74 calories, 2 g total fat, 1 g saturated fat, 3 mg cholesterol, 298 mg sodium, 13 g carbohydrate, 2 g fiber, 3 g protein.

If you prefer a smooth borscht, simply mash or puree half of the mixture before serving.

STIR-FRIED ASPARAGUS AND MUSHROOMS

⅓ cup water
1 teaspoon cornstarch
½ teaspoon instant chicken
   bouillon granules
¼ teaspoon dried thyme,
   crushed
1 dried tomato, finely snipped
   Nonstick spray coating
1 pound fresh asparagus,
   cleaned and cut into 1-inch
   pieces (3 cups)
1½ cups sliced fresh mushrooms
   (4 ounces)

In a small bowl stir together water, cornstarch, chicken bouillon granules, thyme, and snipped dried tomato. Set aside.

Spray a large skillet with nonstick spray coating. Preheat over medium heat. Stir-fry asparagus in the hot skillet for 4 minutes. Add the mushrooms; stir-fry for 1½ minutes more.

Stir cornstarch mixture; add to vegetables in skillet. Cook and stir till thickened and bubbly. Cook and stir for 2 minutes more. Serve immediately. Makes 4 servings.

Nutrition Information Per Serving:
36 calories, 1 g total fat, 0 g saturated fat, 0 mg cholesterol, 113 mg sodium, 6 g carbohydrate, 2 g fiber, 3 g protein.

This savory stir-fry is seasoned with dried thyme, but dill or basil would be equally tasty.

MAPLE-FLAVORED PARSNIPS

The sweet nutty flavor of parsnips goes well with the simple maple glaze. Serve with lean roasted pork.

3 **cups thinly sliced parsnips**
   and/or carrots
2 **tablespoons maple-flavored**
   syrup
1 **tablespoon prepared**
   butter-flavored mix
1 **tablespoon snipped chives**
   (optional)

In a large saucepan with steamer rack, steam sliced parsnips or carrots about 8 minutes or till just tender. Drain parsnips and return to pan without the steamer rack. Stir in syrup and butter-flavored mix. Cook and stir till parsnips are coated and heated through. Sprinkle with snipped chives, if desired. Makes 4 servings.

Nutrition Information Per Serving:
45 calories, 0 g total fat, 0 g saturated fat, 0 mg cholesterol, 25 mg sodium, 11 g carbohydrate, 2 g fiber, 1 g protein.

MICROWAVE MAGIC

Hocus Pocus, press a few buttons, and 1 minute later your microwave melts margarine right before your eyes. Is it magic? No. Is it convenient? Yes. And here are a few other tricks you can pull out of your microwave oven to help you save time in the kitchen. These tips were tested using 600- to 700-watt ovens, so if your oven has fewer watts, you may need to increase the cooking time. Don't forget to use only microwave-safe dishes.

Cooking frozen vegetables: In a 1-quart casserole place 1½ cups loose-pack frozen vegetables and 1 tablespoon water. Cover and cook on 100% power (high) till crisp-tender, stirring once. Drain. Allow 2½ to 3 minutes for broccoli cuts, whole kernel corn, and peas. Allow 4 to 5 minutes for cut green beans, crinkle-cut carrots, cauliflower flowerets, and mixed vegetables.

Baking potatoes: Prick medium potatoes (5 to 6 ounces each) with a fork. Cook, uncovered, on 100% power (high) till almost tender, rearranging once. Allow 5 to 7 minutes for 1 potato and 8 to 10 minutes for 2 potatoes. Let stand 5 minutes.

Melting margarine: Place margarine in a custard cup. Cook, uncovered, on 100% power (high) till melted. Allow 40 to 50 seconds for 2 tablespoons, 45 to 60 seconds for ¼ cup, and 1 to 2 minutes for ½ cup.

Softening margarine: Place margarine in custard cup. Cook, uncovered, on 10% power (low) till softened. Allow 45 seconds for 2 tablespoons and 1 to 1½ minutes for ¼ to ½ cup.

Softening tortillas: Place four 6- to 8-inch flour tortillas between paper towels. Cook on 100% power (high) for 45 to 60 seconds or till softened.

BROCCOLI STALK-CARROT COMBO

2 **medium broccoli stalks**
    (save flowerets for
    another use)
2 **medium carrots**
1 **medium turnip, quartered**
    lengthwise (4 ounces)
1 **cup sliced fresh mushrooms**
1 **cup water**
1 **sprig fresh thyme** *or*
    ¼ **teaspoon dried thyme**
1 **tablespoon snipped parsley**
1 **teaspoon margarine**
    Dash salt
    Dash pepper

Thinly slice broccoli stalks; peel and thinly slice carrots and turnip. (You should have about 3 cups total.) In a medium saucepan combine broccoli, carrot, turnips, mushrooms, water, and thyme. Bring to boiling. Reduce heat; cover and simmer for 5 to 6 minutes or till tender. Drain well. Remove fresh thyme, if using. Add parsley, margarine, salt, and pepper to vegetables. Toss to mix. Makes 4 to 6 servings.

Nutrition Information Per Serving:
48 calories, 1 g total fat, 0 g saturated fat, 0 mg cholesterol, 94 mg sodium, 9 g carbohydrate, 2 g fiber, 3 g protein.

If the broccoli stalks are tough, you may need to peel them with a vegetable peeler or a sharp knife.

GREEN BEANS WITH HORSERADISH SAUCE

1 **pound fresh green beans** *or*
    1 16-ounce package frozen
    cut green beans
½ **cup plain nonfat yogurt**
1 **tablespoon all-purpose flour**
2 **teaspoons prepared**
    horseradish
½ **teaspoon Dijon-style** *or*
    brown mustard
¼ **teaspoon celery seed**

For fresh green beans, wash beans and remove ends and strings from beans. In a medium saucepan cook green beans in a small amount of boiling water for 20 to 25 minutes

or till crisp-tender. (If using frozen green beans, cook according to package directions *except* omit the salt.)

Meanwhile, for sauce, in a small saucepan stir together the yogurt and the flour. Stir in horseradish, mustard, and celery seed. Cook and stir till thickened and bubbly. Cook and stir for 1 minute more. Pour sauce over green beans; toss gently to coat. Makes 4 servings.

Nutrition Information Per Serving:
54 calories, 0 g total fat, 0 g saturated fat, 1 mg cholesterol, 68 mg sodium, 10 g carbohydrate, 2 g fiber, 3 g protein.

Dress up plain green beans with a yogurt-based mixture of horseradish, mustard, and celery seed.

BROCCOLI AND SWEET PEPPERS

12 ounces fresh broccoli
   Nonstick spray coating
 2 large cloves garlic, minced
 1 medium red, yellow, *or* green sweet pepper, cut into ¾-inch pieces
 2 tablespoons water
 ½ teaspoon dried marjoram, crushed
 ⅛ teaspoon salt
 ⅛ teaspoon pepper
 1 teaspoon olive oil *or* cooking oil

Wash broccoli; remove flowerets from stems. Thinly slice the stems into rounds (you should have about 1½ cups). Cut flowerets into smaller flowerets, if necessary (you should have about 2½ cups). Set stems and flowerets aside.

Spray a large skillet with non-stick spray coating. Heat over medium heat. Add garlic; cook and stir for 15 seconds. Add broccoli stems and flowerets, sweet pepper, water, marjoram, salt, and pepper. Cover and cook about 5 minutes or till vegetables are crisp-tender. Sprinkle with oil; toss to coat. Makes 4 servings.

Nutrition Information Per Serving:
42 calories, 2 g total fat, 0 g saturated fat, 0 mg cholesterol, 90 mg sodium, 6 g carbohydrate, 3 g fiber, 3 g protein.

To make this as pretty as possible, use a mixture of red, yellow, and green sweet peppers.

ITALIAN-STYLE PEAS

Bits of orange and thin strips of robust prosciutto flavor frozen peas.

1 10-ounce package frozen peas
¼ cup chopped onion
½ teaspoon finely shredded orange peel
1 medium orange, peeled, sectioned, and cut into ½-inch pieces
1 cup torn leaf lettuce
1 ounce thinly sliced prosciutto *or* fully cooked ham, cut into thin strips
2 teaspoons margarine
 Dash pepper

In a medium saucepan cook peas and onion, covered, in a small amount of boiling water for 5 to 10 minutes or till tender. Drain.

Stir in orange peel, orange pieces, lettuce, prosciutto or ham, margarine, and pepper. Cover; let stand 1 minute. Makes 4 servings.

Nutrition Information Per Serving:
109 calories, 4 g total fat, 0 g saturated fat, 0 mg cholesterol, 210 mg sodium, 13 g carbohydrate, 3 g fiber, 6 g protein.

CARROTS WITH HONEY AND LEMON

This easy blend of honey, lemon juice, and allspice makes these simple carrots spectacular.

3 cups sliced carrots (1 pound)
2 tablespoons honey
2 teaspoons lemon juice
 Dash ground allspice
1 tablespoon snipped parsley

In a medium saucepan cook carrots in a small amount of boiling water about 8 minutes or till crisp-tender. Drain well. Stir together honey, lemon juice, and allspice. Add to carrots; toss to coat. Sprinkle with parsley. Makes 4 servings.

Nutrition Information Per Serving:
81 calories, 0 g total fat, 0 g saturated fat, 0 mg cholesterol, 70 mg sodium, 20 g carbohydrate, 4 g fiber, 1 g protein.

CREAMED SQUASH AND MUSHROOMS

For a colorful side dish, use a combination of sliced yellow summer squash and zucchini.

1 **tablespoon margarine**
1½ **cups sliced yellow summer squash**
2 **cups fresh mushrooms, halved *or* quartered**
¼ **cup reduced-sodium chicken broth**
¼ **cup skim milk**
1 **tablespoon all-purpose flour**
½ **teaspoon fines herbes, crushed, *or* savory, crushed**
 Dash pepper
2 **tablespoons snipped chives**

In a medium saucepan melt margarine. Add summer squash; cook for 2 minutes, stirring occasionally. Add mushrooms; cover and cook over medium-low heat for 3 minutes more.

Meanwhile, combine chicken broth, milk, flour, fines herbes or savory, and pepper. Add to vegetables. Cook and stir till thickened and bubbly. Cook and stir for 1 minute more. Sprinkle with chives. Makes 4 servings.

Nutrition Information Per Serving: 81 calories, 6 g total fat, 1 g saturated fat, 0 mg cholesterol, 101 mg sodium, 6 g carbohydrate, 1 g fiber, 2 g protein.

TATER TOPPINGS

To keep potatoes as fit as Mother Nature made them, be smart about the way you top them. Try these easy healthy tater toppings.

● Italian-style or Mexican-style stewed tomatoes with shredded fat-free or reduced-fat natural cheese
● Nonfat or low-fat cottage cheese with snipped fresh chives
● Spicy mustard or your favorite salsa
● Low-fat chili made with ground turkey or chicken
● Steamed broccoli flowerets or thin carrot strips
● Fat-free dairy sour cream or plain yogurt with capers or sliced green onions
● Fat-free or part-skim ricotta cheese with snipped fresh herbs
● A splash of balsamic vinegar and snipped fresh basil
● A generous squeeze of fresh lemon juice and lots of freshly ground pepper

CARROTS AND PARSNIPS WITH CREAMY MUSTARD SAUCE

3 carrots, thinly sliced
(1½ cups)
2 medium parsnips, thinly
sliced (2½ cups)
½ cup reduced-sodium chicken
broth
2 teaspoons snipped fresh
tarragon *or* ½ teaspoon
dried tarragon, crushed
½ cup plain nonfat yogurt
4 teaspoons all-purpose flour
2 teaspoons Dijon-style
mustard

In a medium saucepan combine carrots, parsnips, chicken broth, and tarragon. Bring to boiling. Reduce heat; cover and simmer for 7 to 9 minutes or till tender.

Meanwhile, in a small bowl, combine yogurt, flour, and mustard. Stir into carrot mixture. Cook and stir till thickened and bubbly. Cook and stir for 1 minute more. Makes 4 servings.

Nutrition Information Per Serving:
132 calories, 1 g total fat, 0 g saturated fat, 1 mg cholesterol, 179 mg sodium, 29 g carbohydrate, 7 g fiber, 4 g protein.

You can slice the carrots and parsnips lickety-split in a food processor using the slicing blade.

STEAMED FENNEL WITH DILL

**2 medium fennel bulbs
    (1 pound)**
**½ cup reduced-sodium chicken
    broth**
1 teaspoon snipped fresh dill *or*
    ⅛ teaspoon dried dillweed
½ cup evaporated skim milk
1 tablespoon cornstarch
    Fresh dill sprigs (optional)

Trim the fennel discarding the woody stems. Cut the fennel into thin slices. In a large saucepan with steamer rack, steam fennel slices, covered, about 12 minutes or till crisp-tender.

Meanwhile, for sauce, in a small saucepan combine broth and dill-weed; bring to boiling. Stir together milk and cornstarch; stir into broth mixture. Cook and stir till thickened and bubbly. Cook and stir for 2 minutes more. To serve, pour sauce over fennel. Garnish with additional dill, if desired. Makes 4 servings.

Nutrition Information Per Serving:
60 calories, 0 g total fat, 0 g saturated fat, 1 mg cholesterol, 131 mg sodium, 12 g carbohydrate, 0 g fiber, 4 g protein.

Kohlrabi with Dill and Chives
Prepare as above *except* substitute 1 pound kohlrabi (peeled and sliced) for the fennel. Steam about 8 minutes or till tender.

Nutrition Information Per Serving:
67 calories, 0 g total fat, 0 g saturated fat, 1 mg cholesterol, 111 mg sodium, 13 g carbohydrate, 2 g fiber, 5 g protein.

If you can't find fresh fennel, try this recipe using 1 pound (3 bulbs) of kohlrabi instead. Steam kohlrabi slices about 8 minutes or till tender.

FEASTING ON FENNEL

Italians eat it raw, dip it in olive oil, and add it to soups, stews, and sauces. This versatile vegetable is fennel, also called Florence fennel or finocchio. Fennel has a creamy white or pale green bulbous base with celerylike stalks. Raw fennel has a light licoricelike flavor and celerylike texture while cooked fennel has a more delicate flavor and softer texture. Look for fennel at your supermarket from September through April. When buying fennel, choose bulbs that are smooth and firm without cracks or blemishes. The stalks should be crisp and the leaves should be bright green and fresh-looking. Once you get it home, store it in a plastic bag in the refrigerator for up to 4 days. Fennel can also be a part of a healthy diet since one-half cup of cooked fennel has only 15 calories.

RED CABBAGE AND APPLES

Choose a tart red apple for this easy side dish, such as Jonathan, Rome Beauty, or Winesap.

3 cups shredded red cabbage
1 large tart red apple, cut into thin wedges
½ of a medium onion, cut into thin wedges
2 tablespoons water
2 tablespoons frozen apple juice concentrate
½ teaspoon instant chicken bouillon granules
¼ teaspoon caraway seed
1 tablespoon red wine vinegar

In a large saucepan combine cabbage, apple, onion, water, apple juice concentrate, chicken granules, and caraway seed. Bring to boiling. Reduce heat; cover and simmer about 5 minutes or till tender. Add wine vinegar; toss to coat. Serve with a slotted spoon. Makes 4 servings.

Nutrition Information Per Serving:
56 calories, 0 g total fat, 0 g saturated fat, 0 mg cholesterol, 116 mg sodium, 14 g carbohydrate, 2 g fiber, 1 g protein.

BALSAMIC GLAZED ONIONS

The sweet-and-sour flavor of these glazed onion wedges pairs nicely with broiled lamb chops.

2 medium onions
2 teaspoons margarine
2 tablespoons balsamic vinegar
1 tablespoon honey
1 tablespoon snipped chives *or* parsley

Cut each onion into 8 wedges. In a large saucepan cook onions in a small amount of boiling water for 5 minutes; drain well.

In a large skillet heat margarine till melted. Add onion wedges. Cook and stir over medium heat about 3 minutes or till onions begin to turn golden.

Meanwhile, stir together the vinegar and honey; pour over onions, stirring to coat evenly. Cook and stir for 1 minute more. Sprinkle with chives or parsley. Makes 4 servings.

Nutrition Information Per Serving:
66 calories, 2 g total fat, 0 g saturated fat, 0 mg cholesterol, 26 mg sodium, 12 g carbohydrate, 1 g fiber, 1 g protein.

CAULIFLOWER WITH PAPRIKA-GARLIC SAUCE

4 cups small cauliflower
   flowerets (about 20 ounces)
2 cloves garlic, minced
1 teaspoon olive oil *or*
   cooking oil
2 tablespoons apple juice
1 tablespoon snipped parsley
1 tablespoon red wine vinegar
1½ teaspoons paprika
⅛ teaspoon salt

In a large saucepan with a steamer rack, steam cauliflower over boiling water, covered, about 8 minutes or till crisp-tender. Meanwhile, for sauce, in a small saucepan cook garlic in hot oil till lightly browned. Remove from heat; stir in apple juice, parsley, vinegar, paprika, and salt. Heat through. Pour the sauce over the hot cauliflower; toss to coat. Makes 4 servings.

Nutrition Information Per Serving:
50 calories, 1 g total fat, 0 g saturated fat, 0 mg cholesterol, 76 mg sodium, 8 g carbohydrate, 3 g fiber, 3 g protein.

This easy, zesty sauce can complement a variety of steamed vegetables such as brussels sprouts, carrots, kohlrabi, and spaghetti squash.

INDIAN-STYLE GREEN BEANS AND CARROTS

¾ pound fresh green beans,
   cut into ¾-inch pieces
2 teaspoons mustard seed
1 teaspoon ground coriander
¼ teaspoon salt
¼ teaspoon ground ginger
¼ teaspoon ground cumin
2 medium carrots, sliced
1 small onion, cut into thin
   wedges
2 teaspoons olive oil *or*
   cooking oil
1 tablespoon lemon juice

In a large saucepan with a steamer rack, steam green beans over boiling water, covered, for 10 minutes.

Meanwhile, stir together mustard seed, coriander, salt, ginger, and cumin; set aside.

Add carrots and onion to beans; steam for 8 to 10 minutes more or till vegetables are crisp-tender.

Meanwhile, in a medium skillet heat oil. Cook spice mixture over medium-high heat till seeds begin to pop. Stir in the hot vegetables and lemon juice; toss to mix. Heat through. Makes 4 servings.

Nutrition Information Per Serving:
96 calories, 3 g total fat, 0 g saturated fat, 0 mg cholesterol, 161 mg sodium, 16 g carbohydrate, 4 g fiber, 3 g protein.

You'll know when the mustard seeds are heated through . . . they'll pop to get your attention.

CURRIED BROCCOLI AND ROTINI

3 ounces rotini *or* gemelli pasta
   (1⅓ cups)
1 tablespoon olive oil *or*
   cooking oil
1 teaspoon curry powder
3 cups broccoli flowerets
½ cup chopped red *or* green
   sweet pepper
½ cup plain low-fat yogurt
⅓ cup reduced-sodium chicken
   broth
4 teaspoons all-purpose flour
1 teaspoon prepared mustard
   Dash salt

Cook pasta according to package directions, *except* omit salt.

Meanwhile, in a large skillet heat oil. Add curry powder and stir-fry over medium-high heat for 1 minute. Add broccoli and sweet pepper; stir-fry for 3 to 4 minutes or till crisp-tender.

For sauce, in a small saucepan, stir together the yogurt, chicken broth, flour, mustard, and salt. Stir into broccoli mixture. Cook and stir till thickened and bubbly. Cook and stir for 1 minute more. Add pasta to broccoli mixture; toss to mix. Heat through. Serve immediately. Makes 4 servings.

Nutrition Information Per Serving:
166 calories, 5 g total fat, 1 g saturated fat, 2 mg cholesterol, 318 mg sodium, 25 g carbohydrate, 2 g fiber, 7 g protein.

Rotini pasta is shaped like corkscrew noodles. Gemelli pasta looks like two strands of pasta twisted together.

FUSILLI WITH REDUCED-FAT PESTO

Cook the pasta just till it is al dente, which means it is tender, but still firm.

1 **10-ounce package frozen chopped spinach, thawed and undrained**
4 **ounces fusilli (rippled fine noodles)** *or* **spaghetti**
½ **of a 20-ounce package frozen crinkle-cut carrots (2½ cups)**
1 **egg white**
2 **tablespoons dried basil, crushed**
1 **tablespoon olive oil** *or* **cooking oil**
2 **cloves garlic**
¼ **cup finely shredded** *or* **grated Parmesan cheese**
Pepper

Cook pasta in boiling water for 7 minutes for the fusilli or for 2 minutes for the spaghetti, stirring occasionally. Add the carrots and cook about 8 minutes more or till pasta is tender but still slightly firm, stirring occasionally.

Meanwhile, for pesto, in a blender container or food processor bowl combine the *undrained* spinach, egg white, basil, oil, and garlic. Cover and blend or process till smooth, stopping occasionally to scrape sides.

In a large colander drain pasta mixture well. Return to hot pan. Add *half* of the pesto to hot pasta mixture. Toss over low heat till pasta is well coated with pesto and heated through. Transfer to serving plates. Sprinkle with Parmesan cheese; season to taste with pepper. Makes 4 servings.

Note: Place remaining pesto in a moisture- and vaporproof freezer container. Seal, label, and freeze up to 3 months. To use, thaw overnight in the refrigerator.

Nutrition Information Per Serving: 188 calories, 4 g total fat, 0 g saturated fat, 5 mg cholesterol, 144 mg sodium, 30 g carbohydrate, 3 g fiber, 8 g protein.

CAULIFLOWER-PASTA MIX

½ **cup tri-colored** *or* **plain rotini (corkscrew macaroni)**

1 **teaspoon snipped fresh rosemary** *or* **¼ teaspoon dried rosemary, crushed**

3 **cups small cauliflower** *or* **broccoflower flowerets**

2 **tablespoons pine nuts**

2 **teaspoons olive oil** *or* **cooking oil**

⅛ **teaspoon garlic salt**

⅛ **teaspoon pepper**

In a large saucepan cook rotini according to package directions *except* omit salt and add rosemary. Add the cauliflower during the last 5 minutes of cooking time. Drain well. Return pasta and cauliflower to saucepan. Add pine nuts, oil, garlic salt, and pepper. Toss to mix. Makes 4 servings.

Nutrition Information Per Serving: 105 calories, 5 g total fat, 1 g saturated fat, 0 mg cholesterol, 71 mg sodium, 12 g carbohydrate, 3 g fiber, 4 g protein.

Get more flavor from your pine nuts by toasting them. Place them in a single layer on a baking sheet in a 350° oven about 5 minutes or till light brown.

BUYING VEGETABLES

Take a few minutes in the produce section and inspect each vegetable before you buy. Look for plump, crisp, brightly colored vegetables that are heavy for their size (this indicates moistness). Avoid vegetables that are bruised, shriveled, moldy, or blemished.

Artichokes: Pick firm globes with large, tightly closed leaves. Darkened leaves do not affect quality.

Asparagus: Choose firm, straight stalks with compact, closed tips. Avoid stalks that are either very thin (less than ⅛ inch) or very thick (more than ½ inch), because they may be stringy.

Broccoli: Look for firm, tender stalks bearing small crisp leaves. The dark green buds should be tightly closed and show no sign of flowering.

Corn: Check for bright, green husks and well-filled even rows of plump kernels.

Green beans: Buy long pods that snap crisply when you bend them.

Mushrooms: Pick plump, firm mushrooms with closed caps. Avoid open caps or mushrooms with blemishes.

Potatoes: Find firm, smooth spuds with shallow eyes. Don't buy potatoes with sprouts or green patches.

GREEK SPINACH AND RICE

To use half a package of the frozen spinach, place the unwrapped spinach in a microwave-safe dish and cook on 30% power (medium-low) for 2 to 4 minutes or just till soft enough to cut in half with a sharp knife. Rewrap one half and return to freezer. Continue to cook the remaining half on 30% power for 3 to 5 minutes more or till thawed.

1 **cup water**
1 **medium onion, finely chopped (½ cup)**
2 **cloves garlic, minced**
1 **teaspoon dried oregano, crushed**
1 **teaspoon instant chicken bouillon granules**
½ **teaspoon finely shredded lemon peel** *or* **1 tablespoon lemon juice**
⅛ **teaspoon pepper**
½ **cup long grain rice**
½ **of a 10-ounce package frozen chopped spinach, thawed and drained**
Lemon peel strips (optional)

In a medium saucepan combine water, onion, garlic, oregano, chicken bouillon granules, lemon peel or juice, and pepper. Bring to boiling. Stir in rice; reduce heat. Cover and simmer for 10 minutes.

Stir in spinach. Cover and cook for 5 to 10 minutes more or till rice is tender and liquid is absorbed. Stir lightly with a fork before serving. Garnish with lemon peel strips, if desired. Makes 4 servings.

Nutrition Information Per Serving:
113 calories, 0 g total fat, 0 g saturated fat, 0 mg cholesterol, 251 mg sodium, 24 g carbohydrate, 2 g fiber, 3 g protein.

SOUTHWESTERN BLACK-EYED PEA SALAD

If you can't find frozen black-eyed peas, use canned ones, but be sure to rinse them well to remove excess sodium.

MAKE AHEAD

2 cups frozen loose-pack black-eyed peas
1 cup frozen whole kernel corn
2 medium tomatoes, seeded and chopped (1 cup)
¾ cup chopped green pepper
⅔ cup nonfat Italian salad dressing
2 tablespoons snipped parsley
1 jalapeño pepper, finely chopped
1 teaspoon ground cumin
Lettuce leaves (optional)

In a medium saucepan cook black-eyed peas in boiling water for 12 minutes. Add corn. Cook about 5 minutes more or till vegetables are tender. Drain.

In a medium bowl combine drained black-eyed peas and corn, tomatoes, green pepper, Italian dressing, parsley, jalapeño pepper, and cumin. Mix well. Cover and chill for 4 to 24 hours. Serve on lettuce-lined plates, if desired. Makes 6 to 8 servings

Nutrition Information Per Serving: 117 calories, 1 g total fat, 0 g saturated fat, 0 mg cholesterol, 385 mg sodium, 23 g carbohydrate, 5 g fiber, 6 g protein.

THE FROZEN FACTS ABOUT VEGETABLES

To keep up with today's hectic pace and healthy lifestyle, look no further than your grocer's freezer case for frozen vegetables. They are quick and easy to prepare and packed with as much or more nutrition than fresh vegetables. And, you'll find a huge variety to choose from with all different package sizes to fit anyone's needs. To keep the fat, calories, and sodium in line, avoid frozen vegetables in sauces and butter. Here are a few more good reasons to consider eating frozen vegetables.

Frozen vegetables are often picked and frozen within 4 to 6 hours, locking in vitamins and freshness.

Frozen vegetables are convenient and easy to prepare because little to no preparation time is required.

Frozen vegetables are a good value because there's more usable vegetable per pound than fresh.

Frozen vegetables reduce waste because every vegetable in the package is usable.

Frozen vegetables are consistently priced from season to season.

Frozen vegetables are available year-round in your grocer's freezer case.

BRILLIANT
BREAKFASTS

INDIVIDUAL ITALIAN EGGS

1 small zucchini, halved
    lengthwise and thinly
    sliced
1 medium red onion, chopped
    (½ cup)
½ cup chopped red *or*
    green sweet pepper
2 cloves garlic, minced
2 teaspoons olive oil *or*
    cooking oil
6 egg whites
1 egg
1 cup skim milk
¼ teaspoon dried Italian
    seasoning, crushed
¼ cup shredded part-skim
    mozzarella cheese
    (1 ounce)

In a medium skillet cook zucchini, onion, sweet pepper, and garlic in hot oil till onion is tender.

In a medium bowl combine egg whites, whole egg, milk, and Italian seasoning; mix well. Stir in cooked mixture. Pour into four individual (about 4½-inches in diameter) quiche dishes.

Bake in a 350° oven for 15 to 20 minutes or till set. Sprinkle each serving with mozzarella cheese. Let stand 5 minutes before serving. Makes 4 servings.

Nutrition Information Per Serving:
114 calories, 5 g total fat, 2 g saturated fat, 58 mg cholesterol, 164 mg sodium, 6 g carbohydrate, 1 g fiber, 11 g protein.

To keep the baking time short, this quiche-style breakfast bakes in individual dishes.

STUFFED FRENCH TOAST

Don't be fooled by the rich-tasting, mixture that fills each piece of this French toast. It's a guilt-free mixture of fat-free cream cheese product and fruit.

8 1-inch thick diagonally cut slices French bread
1 8-ounce can pineapple tidbits (juice pack)
1 8-ounce container fat-free cream cheese product
1 tablespoon apricot all-fruit spread
2 teaspoons sugar
½ teaspoon vanilla
2 egg whites
½ cup skim milk
⅔ cup apricot all-fruit spread
⅛ teaspoon ground nutmeg
Nonstick spray coating

Using a serrated bread knife, cut a slit through the top of each slice of bread to form a pocket. Set aside.

Drain the pineapple tidbits reserving juice. For filling, in a medium bowl combine cream cheese product, *half* of the pineapple tidbits, 1 tablespoon all-fruit spread, sugar, and vanilla. Stir till well mixed. Spoon *1 rounded tablespoon* of the filling in the pocket of each slice of bread.

In a shallow bowl combine egg whites, skim milk, and *2 tablespoons* of the reserved pineapple juice. Dip stuffed bread slices in egg mixture just long enough to coat both sides.

Spray a baking sheet with non-stick spray coating. Place the bread slices on the baking sheet. Bake in a 450° oven for 8 minutes. Turn the slices over. Bake for 7 minutes more.

Meanwhile, in a small saucepan combine remaining pineapple, *2 tablespoons* of the remaining reserved pineapple juice, ⅔ cup all-fruit spread, and nutmeg. Cook and stir over medium heat just till fruit spread melts. Serve warm with the French toast. Makes 4 servings.

Nutrition Information Per Serving: 472 calories, 3 g total fat, 1 g saturated fat, 10 mg cholesterol, 835 mg sodium, 90 g carbohydrate, 3 g fiber, 22 g protein.

TEX-MEX TURKEY BREAKFAST SAUSAGE

Nonstick spray coating
1 egg white, slightly beaten
4 green onions, finely chopped
    (¼ cup)
¼ cup finely chopped red *or*
    green sweet pepper
¼ cup coarsely shredded carrot
3 tablespoons quick-cooking
    rolled oats
1 large clove garlic, minced
¼ teaspoon salt
¼ teaspoon ground cumin
¼ teaspoon dried oregano,
    crushed
¼ teaspoon ground black
    pepper

⅛ teaspoon ground red pepper
   Dash ground cloves
½ pound lean ground raw
   turkey breast

Ask your butcher to grind 8 ounces lean turkey breast to use in these well-seasoned sausage patties.

Spray the unheated rack of a broiler pan or a baking pan with nonstick spray coating; set aside.

In a medium bowl combine egg white, chopped green onion, chopped sweet pepper, carrot, oats, garlic, salt, cumin, oregano, black pepper, ground red pepper, and cloves. Add turkey; mix well.

Shape mixture into eight 2-inch patties. Place patties on the prepared pan. Bake in a 450° oven for 10 to 15 minutes or till golden brown and no longer pink. Makes 8 servings.

Nutrition Information Per Serving:
43 calories, 1 g total fat, 0 g saturated fat, 12 mg cholesterol, 92 mg sodium, 2 g carbohydrate, 0 g fiber, 6 g protein.

HONEY-APPLE PANCAKES

1¼ cups all-purpose flour
2 teaspoons baking powder
¼ teaspoon salt
¼ teaspoon apple pie spice
⅛ teaspoon baking soda
1 beaten egg
¾ cup apple juice
2 tablespoons honey
1 tablespoon cooking oil
   Nonstick spray coating

In a medium bowl stir together flour, baking powder, salt, apple pie spice, and baking soda. In a small bowl stir together egg, apple juice, honey, and oil; add all at once to the flour mixture, stirring till mixed but still slightly lumpy.

Spray a cold nonstick griddle or heavy skillet with nonstick spray coating. Preheat griddle or skillet over medium heat.

For each pancake, pour about ¼ *cup* of the batter onto the hot griddle or heavy skillet. Cook for 2 to 3 minutes or till pancakes have a bubbly surface and slightly dry edges. Turn pancakes; cook for 2 to 3 minutes more or till golden brown. Makes about eight 4-inch pancakes.

Nutrition Information Per Serving:
121 calories, 3 g total fat, 1 g saturated fat, 27 mg cholesterol, 93 mg sodium, 21 g carbohydrate, 1 g fiber, 3 g protein.

Serve these golden griddle cakes with honey, reduced-calorie syrup, or fresh fruit.

BAKED BREAKFAST APPLES

As one of our taste testers said, "it's almost too good!" And you'll think so, too. If you don't try it for breakfast, try it for dessert (it makes 4 dessert servings).

2 medium apples, cut into bite-size chunks
2 tablespoons snipped dates
½ teaspoon ground cinnamon
½ cup apple juice
2 tablespoons raspberry all-fruit spread
¼ cup reduced-fat granola

In two individual casseroles combine the apples and dates. Sprinkle with cinnamon. Pour apple juice over apple mixture.

Bake, covered, in a 350º oven for 20 to 25 minutes or till apples are slightly tender.

Meanwhile, in a small saucepan, heat all-fruit spread till melted. Drizzle fruit spread over apple mixture and sprinkle with granola. Serve warm. Makes 2 servings.

Nutrition Information Per Serving:
229 calories, 1 g total fat, 0 g saturated fat, 0 mg cholesterol, 28 mg sodium, 57 g carbohydrate, 3 g fiber, 2 g protein.

USING EGG SUBSTITUTES

You can enjoy tasty low-cholesterol versions of your favorite omelets, custards, and other egg-based foods by incorporating egg substitutes into your cooking. These eggs-in-disguise are based mostly on egg whites and contain less fat than whole eggs and no cholesterol. Besides obvious egg dishes like omelets, try egg substitutes in yeast breads, muffins, cakes, cookies, casseroles, sauces, puddings, and custards. Avoid using egg substitutes in cream puffs or popovers because they won't puff or pop. Check the package directions before using any egg substitute.

You can make your own homemade egg substitute by using 2 egg whites for each whole egg called for in a recipe. If the recipe requires a lot of eggs or it needs a little richness or color, then use 2 egg whites and 1 whole egg for every 2 whole eggs.

STRAWBERRY-PAPAYA BREAKFAST SHAKE

½ **cup skim milk**
½ **cup plain nonfat yogurt**
½ **cup fresh strawberries,
    hulled**
½   **of a medium papaya, seeded,
    peeled, and chopped
    (about ¾ cup)**
1 **tablespoon honey**
3 **large ice cubes** *or* ⅓ **cup
    crushed ice**

In a blender container combine skim milk, plain yogurt, strawberries, papaya, and honey. Cover and blend till smooth. With the blender running, add ice cubes, one at a time, through the opening in lid. Blend till smooth. Pour into tall glasses; serve immediately. Makes 2 (10-ounce) servings.

Nutrition Information Per Serving:
220 calories, 1 g total fat, 0 g saturated fat, 2 mg cholesterol, 91 mg sodium, 48 g carbohydrate, 5 g fiber, 6 g protein.

Wouldn't this make a nifty take-along breakfast in the car on the way to work or school? Yes!

THE MANY FACES OF MARGARINE

The old tub of margarine just ain't what it used to be. Before it was easy to decide what to spread on your morning toast. Now the choices are endless, which gives you more variety, but more confusion, too. Here are the descriptions for some of the margarine products to help ease your bewilderment. Whichever you choose, use them sparingly.

Regular margarines: Must contain 80 percent fat and most are made with a single vegetable oil. Sticks of regular margarine are available salted and unsalted. By purchasing unsalted margarine and adding a just a touch of salt for flavor is one easy way to reduce sodium in recipes.

Diet margarines: Contain half of the fat of regular margarine and more water. These are not recommended for cooking or baking unless the recipe has been developed using these products.

Vegetable oil spreads: Contain more fat than diet margarine and less fat than regular margarine. These are not recommended for cooking or baking unless the recipe has been developed using these products.

BROCCOLI AND TOFU QUICHE

Reduced-fat cheese and tofu make for a low-fat, low-cholesterol quiche filling that tastes every bit as good as the real thing.

½ **of a 10-ounce package frozen chopped broccoli**
Nonstick spray coating
2 **tablespoons toasted wheat bran**
½ **cup shredded reduced-fat mozzarella *or* Swiss cheese (2 ounces)**
6 **ounces tofu**
½ **cup skim milk**
2 **egg whites**
1 **egg**
¼ **cup grated Parmesan cheese**
4 **green onions, sliced (¼ cup)**
1 **tablespoon all-purpose flour**
1 **teaspoon dried dill *or* basil, crushed**
Fresh dill sprigs (optional)

In a medium saucepan, cook broccoli in a small amount of boiling water, about 5 minutes or till tender. Drain and set aside.

Meanwhile, spray a 9-inch pie plate with nonstick spray coating. Sprinkle the bottom evenly with wheat bran. Sprinkle shredded mozzarella or Swiss cheese evenly over wheat bran.

For filling, in a blender container or food processor bowl combine tofu, milk, egg white, egg, *half* of the Parmesan cheese, green onion, flour, and dill or basil. Cover and blend or process till smooth. Stir in the broccoli. Pour the filling over the cheese in the pie plate. Sprinkle with the remaining Parmesan cheese.

Bake in a 375° oven for 25 to 30 minutes or till set in center. Let stand 5 minutes before serving. Cut into wedges to serve. Garnish with fresh dill, if desired. Makes 4 to 6 servings.

Nutrition Information Per Serving:
153 calories, 7 g total fat, 3 g saturated fat, 67 mg cholesterol, 267 mg sodium, 9 g carbohydrate, 3 g fiber, 15 g protein.

BREAKFAST COUSCOUS
WITH ORANGES AND CRANBERRIES

Special couscous topped with this honey-sweetened fruit sauce offers a new twist on hot breakfast cereal.

1 **cup skim milk**
¼ **teaspoon ground cinnamon**
  Dash ground nutmeg
1 **cup couscous**
2 **tablespoons dried currants**
⅓ **cup orange juice**
¾ **cup fresh cranberries**
2 **tablespoons honey**
2 **tablespoons water**
1 **11-ounce can mandarin orange sections, drained**
1 **tablespoon slivered almonds, toasted**

In a medium saucepan combine skim milk, cinnamon, and nutmeg. Bring to boiling over medium heat. Add couscous and currants. Cover; remove from heat. Let stand for 5 minutes. Stir in orange juice. Fluff with a fork.

Meanwhile, in a small skillet toss together cranberries, honey, and water. Cook over low heat for 4 to 5 minutes or till the cranberry skins begin to pop. Remove from heat. Gently stir in orange sections and almonds.

To serve, spoon warm couscous into individual serving bowls. Top each serving with warm cranberry-orange mixture. Serve immediately. Makes 4 servings.

Nutrition Information Per Serving:
303 calories, 1 g total fat, 0 g saturated fat, 1 mg cholesterol, 43 mg sodium, 65 g carbohydrate, 9 g fiber, 9 g protein.

DRIED PEAR AND CRANBERRY MUESLI

This European version of granola is a welcome change from dry cereal and milk. You can make it ahead by combining all the ingredients, except the milk and yogurt, and storing them in an airtight container.

⅔ **cup quick-cooking oats**
2 **tablespoons toasted wheat germ**
1 **cup skim milk**
¼ **cup dried pear *or* apple slices, snipped**
2 **tablespoons dried cranberries *or* snipped dried apricots**
2 **tablespoons slivered almonds**
1 **tablespoon brown sugar**
¼ **teaspoon ground cinnamon**

¼ **cup plain nonfat *or* vanilla low-fat yogurt**

In a bowl combine uncooked oats, wheat germ, milk, pears or apples, cranberries or apricots, almonds, brown sugar, and cinnamon. Mix well. Let stand for 10 to 15 minutes. Serve in bowls with yogurt. Makes 2 servings.

Nutrition Information Per Serving: 346 calories, 7 g total fat, 1 g saturated fat, 3 mg cholesterol, 91 mg sodium, 60 g carbohydrate, 4 g fiber, 14 g protein.

A.M. FIBER

One of the easiest ways to get more fiber into your diet is at your morning meal with a healthy dose of cereal, whole grain bread, or fresh juicy fruits. Take a good look at the foods below to help you make smart fiber-rich choices.

Cereals
Whole bran (⅓ cup) ....8.5 g
100% bran (½ cup)............................8.4 g
40% bran flakes (¾ cup) ....4.0 g
Granola, homemade (¼ cup)..............3.0 g
Raisin bran (½ cup) ....3.0 g
Oatmeal (¾ cup cooked) ....3.0 g
Shredded wheat (1 biscuit)................2.2 g
Wheat flakes (1 cup) ....2.0 g

Breads
Whole wheat bread (1 slice)..............2.7 g
Bran muffin, homemade.....................2.5 g

Plain English muffin (1 whole) ....1.5 g
Plain bagel (1 whole)..........................1.2 g
White bread (1 slice)...........................0.6 g

Fruit
Dried prunes (½ cup)..........................5.5 g
Raisins (½ cup)..................................3.8 g
Orange (1)...3.1 g
Apple (1 with skin)..............................3.0 g
Strawberries (½ cup) ....1.9 g
Banana (1)...1.8 g
Cantaloupe, cubed (1 cup) ....1.0 g
Grapefruit (½)......................................1.0 g

WHOLE WHEAT PANCAKES

1 cup soft bread crumbs
    (use white *or* soft wheat
    bread)
⅓ cup nonfat dry milk powder
⅔ cup hot water
1 tablespoon cooking oil
1 beaten egg
⅓ cup whole wheat flour
¾ teaspoon baking powder
⅛ teaspoon salt
    Nonstick spray coating

In a medium mixing bowl stir together bread crumbs and milk powder. Stir in the hot water and cooking oil. Let mixture stand for 5 minutes. Stir in the beaten egg, whole wheat flour, baking powder, and salt.

Spray a griddle or skillet with nonstick coating; heat griddle over medium heat.

For each pancake, pour 2 to 3 tablespoons batter onto hot griddle. Cook till pancakes are golden, turning to cook the second side when pancakes have a bubbly surface and slightly dry edges. Makes ten 4-inch pancakes.

Nutrition Information Per Pancake: 55 calories, 2 g total fat, 0 g saturated fat, 22 mg cholesterol, 70 mg sodium, 6 g carbohydrate, 1 g fiber, 2 g protein.

To keep the first pancakes warm while you finish cooking the rest, arrange the pancakes on a baking sheet and place them in a 300° oven.

ROSEMARY AND POTATO SKILLET

8 ounces tiny new red potatoes,
cut into ¼-inch-thick slices
1 cup fresh asparagus spears
cut into ½-inch pieces
Nonstick spray coating
1½ cups frozen egg product,
thawed
1 tablespoon snipped parsley
1 teaspoon snipped fresh
rosemary *or* ½ teaspoon
dried rosemary, crushed
¼ to ½ teaspoon onion powder
¼ teaspoon salt
¼ teaspoon pepper
1 large tomato, seeded and
coarsely chopped
1 tablespoon finely shredded *or*
grated Parmesan cheese

In a large nonstick skillet cook potatoes in a small amount of boiling water, covered, for 5 minutes. Add the asparagus; cover and cook for 5 to 7 minutes more or till the vegetables are tender. Drain. Dry the skillet.

Spray the skillet with nonstick spray coating. Return vegetables to skillet. In a medium bowl combine egg product, parsley, rosemary, onion powder, salt, and pepper. Pour into skillet over vegetables. Cook over medium heat. As mixture sets, run a spatula around the edge of the skillet, lifting egg mixture to allow uncooked portions to flow underneath. Continue cooking and lifting edges till egg mixture is almost set (surface will be moist).

Remove skillet from heat. Cover and let stand for 3 to 4 minutes or till top is set. Spoon onto plates. Top with chopped tomato and sprinkle with Parmesan cheese. Makes 4 servings.

Nutrition Information Per Serving:
163 calories, 4 g total fat, 1 g saturated fat, 2 mg cholesterol, 348 mg sodium, 17 g carbohydrate, 2 g fiber, 15 g protein.

TOMATO AND BASIL FRITTATA

If you don't have an oven-going skillet for this recipe, simply cover the handle of an 8-inch skillet with foil.

5 egg whites
1 egg
1 tablespoon snipped fresh
  basil *or* ½ teaspoon dried
  basil, crushed
⅛ teaspoon salt
  Dash pepper
  Nonstick spray coating
½ cup chopped fresh spinach
2 green onions, sliced
  (2 tablespoons)
1 clove garlic, minced
1 small tomato, chopped
¼ cup shredded reduced-fat
  cheddar cheese (1 ounce)

In a medium bowl lightly beat together egg whites and whole egg. Stir in basil, salt, and pepper; set aside.

Spray a cold 8-inch oven-going skillet with nonstick coating. Preheat the skillet over medium heat. Add spinach, green onion, and garlic. Cook for 1 to 2 minutes or till spinach begins to wilt. Remove skillet from heat; drain, if necessary.

Pour egg mixture over spinach mixture in the skillet. Bake, uncovered, in a 350° oven for 6 to 8 minutes or till eggs are set. Sprinkle with chopped tomato and cheese. Bake for 1 to 2 minutes more or till the cheese melts. Cut the frittata into wedges to serve. Makes 2 servings.

Nutrition Information Per Serving:
149 calories, 6 g total fat, 2 g saturated fat, 117 mg cholesterol, 428 mg sodium, 5 g carbohydrate, 1 g fiber, 17 g protein.

HOMEMADE

BREADS

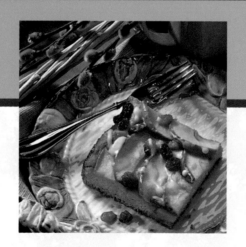

LEMONY STAR FRUIT KUCHEN

 45

½ **cup all-purpose flour**
½ **cup yellow cornmeal**
⅓ **cup quick-cooking rolled oats**
1 **teaspoon baking powder**
⅛ **teaspoon baking soda**
2 **egg whites**
½ **cup plain nonfat yogurt**
⅓ **cup packed brown sugar**
2 **tablespoons dark molasses**
2 **tablespoons margarine,
    melted**
1 **teaspoon finely shredded
    lemon peel**
  Nonstick spray coating
1 **large star fruit (6 ounces),
    cut into 12 slices**
2 **teaspoons granulated sugar**

In a large bowl, stir together flour, cornmeal, oats, baking powder, and baking soda. In another bowl stir together egg whites, yogurt, brown sugar, molasses, melted margarine, and lemon peel. Add egg white mixture to flour mixture, stirring just till combined.

Spray an 8-inch round quiche pan or cake pan with nonstick spray coating. Spread batter into prepared pan. Gently press star fruit slices into batter.

Bake in a 350° oven about 30 minutes or till a toothpick inserted near center comes out clean. Lightly sprinkle with granulated sugar. Cool slightly in pan on a wire rack. Cut into wedges. Serve warm. Makes 8 servings.

Nutrition Information Per Serving:
166 calories, 4 g total fat, 1 g saturated fat, 0 mg cholesterol, 78 mg sodium, 30 g carbohydrate, 1 g fiber, 4 g protein.

Star fruit, sometimes called carambola, is named for its star-shaped slices. Its slightly tart flavor tastes like a combination of lemon, pineapple, and apple.

CRANBERRY-OAT MINI-MUFFINS

If you don't have a miniature muffin pan, this recipe will make 6 full-size muffins. Bake them in a 400° oven for 20 to 25 minutes.

Nonstick spray coating
¾ **cup all-purpose flour**
¼ **cup oat bran**
1 **teaspoon baking powder**
   Dash salt
1 **slightly beaten egg white**
½ **cup milk**
3 **tablespoons sugar**
2 **tablespoons cooking oil**
⅓ **cup chopped dried**
   cranberries, chopped
   raisins, or dried currants
1 **tablespoon sugar**
⅛ **teaspoon ground cinnamon**

Spray eighteen 1¾-inch muffin cups with nonstick spray coating; set aside.

In a large bowl stir together flour, oat bran, baking powder, and salt. Make a well in the center of the dry ingredients.

In another bowl combine the egg white, milk, 3 tablespoons sugar, and oil. Add egg mixture all at once to dry ingredients. Stir just till moistened, (batter should be lumpy). Fold cranberries, raisins, or currants into batter. Spoon batter into prepared muffin cups filling each about ¾ full.

Bake in a 400° oven for 12 to 15 minutes or till golden. Cool in pans on a wire rack for 5 minutes; then remove muffins from pans. Serve warm. Makes 18.

Nutrition Information Per Muffin:
53 calories, 2 g total fat, 0 g saturated fat, 0 mg cholesterol, 14 mg sodium, 8 g carbohydrate, 0 g fiber, 1 g protein.

MUSTARD FRENCH BREAD

Here's a simple spread to dress up French bread in a flash. It makes a tasty snack, too.

1 tablespoon reduced-calorie
  mayonnaise *or*
  salad dressing
1 teaspoon Dijon-style mustard
2 slices French bread
1 tablespoon snipped parsley
2 teaspoons grated Parmesan
  cheese

In a small bowl combine the mayonnaise or salad dressing and the mustard. Spread onto one side of the bread slices. Sprinkle tops with parsley and Parmesan cheese.

Arrange bread slices, coated side up, on the unheated rack of a broiler pan. Broil about 5 inches from the heat for 3 to 4 minutes or till golden. Serve warm. Makes 2 servings.

Nutrition Information Per Serving:
136 calories, 5 g total fat, 1 g saturated fat, 2 mg cholesterol, 351 mg sodium, 19 g carbohydrate, 1 g fiber, 4 g protein.

QUICK-THAW BREAD DOUGH

The next time you use frozen bread dough and don't have time to thaw it overnight, turn to your microwave oven. First, try this test to see if you can thaw frozen bread dough in your microwave oven. Place 2 tablespoons cold stick margarine (not corn oil spread) in a custard cup in the center of your oven. Cook, uncovered, on 10% power (low) for 4 minutes. If the margarine completely melts, you cannot thaw frozen bread dough in your microwave oven. If it doesn't completely melt, then thaw dough by cooking on 10% power (low) for 15 to 17 minutes or till thawed, rotating dough occasionally.

GREEN ONION AND BASIL BISCUITS

1 cup all-purpose flour
1 green onion, sliced
   (1 tablespoon)
1½ teaspoons baking powder
1 teaspoon sugar
   Dash salt
¼ teaspoon dried basil, crushed
⅓ cup skim milk
2 tablespoons cooking oil
4 ounces fat-free cream cheese
   product

In a medium bowl combine flour, green onion, baking powder, sugar, basil, and salt.

In a small bowl stir together milk and oil. Pour over flour mixture; stir just till well mixed.

On a lightly floured surface, knead dough gently for 10 to 12 strokes. Roll or pat dough to ½-inch thickness. Cut with a 2-inch biscuit cutter, dipping cutter into additional flour between cuts. Transfer biscuits to an ungreased baking sheet.

Bake in a 450° oven for 10 to 12 minutes or till golden. Serve biscuits warm with cream cheese product. Makes 8.

Nutrition Information Per Biscuit:
104 calories, 4 g total fat, 1 g saturated fat, 3 mg cholesterol, 108 mg sodium, 13 g carbohydrate, 0 g fiber, 5 g protein.

Any leftover biscuits? Reheat them in your microwave oven on 100% power (high) for 20 to 30 seconds. For best results, cover them with a microwave-safe paper towel.

APPLE BUTTER SWEET ROLLS

Nonstick spray coating
1 **16-ounce loaf frozen sweet bread dough, thawed (see tip, page 194)**
⅓ **cup apple *or* peach butter**
2 **tablespoons dried currants *or* raisins**
⅓ **cup sifted powdered sugar**
½ **teaspoon finely shredded orange peel**
1 **to 2 teaspoons apple *or* orange juice**

Spray twelve 2½-inch muffin cups with nonstick spray coating; set muffin cups aside.

On a lightly floured surface roll thawed dough to a 12x8-inch rectangle. Spread apple butter evenly over dough. Sprinkle with currants or raisins. Roll up, from a long side, jelly-roll style. Pinch seam to seal. Cut into 12 slices. Place rolls, cut side down, in prepared muffin cups. Cover and let rise in a warm place for 15 minutes.

Bake in a 350° oven for 20 minutes or till golden. Remove from pan; place on a wire rack.

For icing, in a small bowl, combine powdered sugar, orange peel, and enough apple or orange juice to make desired consistency. Drizzle icing over rolls. Serve warm. Makes 12.

Nutrition Information Per Roll:
135 calories, 3 g total fat, 0 g saturated fat, 0 mg cholesterol, 195 mg sodium, 24 g carbohydrate, 1 g fiber, 5 g protein.

Frozen bread dough cuts hours of work from these homespun sweet rolls.

Banana Bran Muffins

These moist, flavorful muffins contain little bits of lots of things—raisins, banana, carrot, nuts, and spices.

Nonstick spray coating
¼ cup raisins
¾ cup all-purpose flour
½ cup oat bran
½ cup packed brown sugar
¼ cup rice bran
1 teaspoon baking powder
1 teaspoon ground cinnamon
½ teaspoon baking soda
⅛ teaspoon ground allspice
⅓ cup mashed ripe banana
    (1 medium)
¼ cup skim milk
¼ cup frozen egg substitute,
    thawed, or 2 slightly
    beaten egg whites
2 tablespoons cooking oil
½ teaspoon vanilla
½ cup shredded carrot
¼ cup chopped walnuts

Spray muffin cups with nonstick spray coating or line with paper bake cups. Set aside. Pour enough boiling water over raisins to cover. Let stand 5 minutes; drain well. Set aside.

In a large bowl combine flour, oat bran, brown sugar, rice bran, baking powder, cinnamon, baking soda, and allspice. Make a well in the center.

In a medium bowl combine mashed banana, milk, egg substitute or egg whites, cooking oil, and vanilla. Add all at once to the flour mixture. Stir just till moistened (batter should be lumpy). Fold in raisins, carrot, and nuts. Fill prepared muffin cups ⅔ full.

Bake in a 400° oven for 18 to 20 minutes or till golden. Remove from pans; serve warm. Makes 10 to 12 muffins.

Nutrition Information Per Muffin:
162 calories, 6 g total fat, 1 g saturated fat, 0 mg cholesterol, 105 mg sodium, 28 g carbohydrate, 2 g fiber, 4 g protein.

PARMESAN CORNBREAD PUFFS

Nonstick spray coating
½ cup all-purpose flour
⅓ cup yellow cornmeal
4 teaspoons sugar
1 teaspoon baking powder
Dash salt
1 slightly beaten egg white
⅓ cup skim milk
2 tablespoons cooking oil
2 tablespoons grated Parmesan
cheese

Spray twelve 1¾-inch muffin cups with nonstick coating; set aside.

In a large bowl stir together flour, cornmeal, sugar, baking powder, and salt. Beat together egg white, milk, and oil. Add to flour mixture and stir just till smooth. Spoon into prepared muffin cups, filling about ¾ full.

Bake in a 425° oven for 10 to 12 minutes or till golden. Remove from pan; cool on a wire rack 5 minutes. Place cheese in a plastic bag. Add warm puffs, a few at a time; toss to coat with cheese. Serve warm. Makes 12.

Nutrition Information Per Puff:
69 calories, 3 g total fat, 1 g saturated fat, 1 mg cholesterol, 40 mg sodium, 9 g carbohydrate, 0 g fiber, 2 g protein.

These light-tasting cornmeal muffins are coated with grated Parmesan cheese after they are baked. Serve them with a bowl of chili or hearty soup.

NONSTICK SPRAY SECRETS

Nonstick cooking spray is a handy kitchen staple for the time-pressed and health-conscious cook. What makes this simple spray work like magic? Vegetable oils and lecithin (from soybeans) prevent sticking and alcohol helps the spray action (but evaporates on contact). And the environment can rest at ease because these sprays are propelled by natural hydrocarbons, not chlorofluorocarbons that are harmful to the ozone layer. Here are a few secrets for successful spraying.

● Spray sparingly. Using a 1¼-second spray is like using 1 tablespoon of cooking oil, margarine, butter, or shortening.

● Hold the pan you are spraying over your sink so you don't make the floor or counter slippery.

● Spray only onto cold baking pans or skillets because nonstick spray coating can burn or smoke if sprayed onto hot surfaces.

● Spray kitchen shears or scissors with nonstick cooking spray when snipping dried fruit. This prevents them from sticking to the fruit.

● Make grilling cleanup easier by spraying your cold barbecue rack with nonstick spray before firing up the coals.

MAPLE-WHOLE WHEAT BATTER ROLLS

Nonstick spray coating
1½ **cups all-purpose flour**
1 **package quick-rising active**
     dry yeast
1½ **cups water**
¼ **cup maple-flavored syrup** *or*
     honey
1 **tablespoon margarine**
½ **teaspoon salt**
1½ **cups whole wheat flour**
1 **tablespoon skim milk**

Spray twelve 2½-inch muffin cups with nonstick spray coating; set muffin cups aside.

In a large bowl stir together the all-purpose flour and yeast. Heat water, maple-flavored syrup or honey, margarine, and salt to 125° to 130°; add to flour mixture. Beat with an electric mixer on low to medium speed for 30 seconds, scraping sides of bowl. Then beat on high speed for 2 minutes. Beat or stir in the whole wheat flour. Spoon batter into muffin cups. Cover and let rest in a warm place for 15 minutes.

Brush tops lightly with milk. Bake in a 400° oven about 20 minutes or till brown and rolls sound hollow when tapped. Remove from pans; cool slightly on a wire rack. Serve warm. Makes 12.

Nutrition Information Per Roll:
136 calories, 2 g total fat, 0 g saturated fat, 0 mg cholesterol, 116 mg sodium, 27 g carbohydrate, 2 g fiber, 4 g protein.

Serve these slightly sweet rolls with a main dish salad or set them out for breakfast with your favorite fruit preserves.

45

OVERNIGHT APPLE-ORANGE COFFEE CAKE

2 **cups all-purpose flour**
1 **package active dry yeast**
1 **teaspoon baking powder**
½ **teaspoon ground cardamom**
¾ **cup water**
¼ **cup sugar**
¼ **cup cooking oil**
¼ **teaspoon salt**
1 **egg white**
1 **tablespoon finely shredded orange peel**
3 **medium apples, cored and thinly sliced (3 cups)**
¼ **cup raisins**
2 **tablespoons frozen orange juice concentrate *or* apple juice concentrate, thawed**
2 **tablespoons dark corn syrup**
Orange Glaze

Lightly grease a 13x9x2-inch baking pan; set aside.

In a large bowl combine *1 cup* of the flour, the yeast, baking powder, and cardamom. In a small saucepan heat water, sugar, oil, and salt till warm (120° to 130°). Add to flour mixture along with egg white. Beat with an electric mixer on low speed for 30 seconds, scraping bowl frequently. Beat on high speed for 3 minutes. Using a spoon stir in orange peel and remaining flour till well mixed. Cover; let dough rest for 5 to 10 minutes while preparing apples. In a medium bowl combine apple slices, raisins, juice concentrate, and corn syrup. Cover and refrigerate overnight.

Spoon dough into prepared pan; spread evenly. Cover and refrigerate overnight.

About 1 hour before serving, remove dough and apple mixture from refrigerator. Spoon apple mixture over dough. Bake in a 375° oven for 30 to 35 minutes or till golden and apples are tender. Cool slightly in pan on rack. Drizzle with Orange Glaze. Serve warm. Makes 12 to 16 servings.

Orange Glaze: In a medium bowl combine ½ cup sifted *powdered sugar* and ½ teaspoon finely shredded *orange peel*. Add 2 to 3 teaspoons *orange juice* to make glaze of drizzling consistency.

Nutrition Information Per Serving: 168 calories, 5 g total fat, 1 g saturated fat, 0 mg cholesterol, 58 mg sodium, 29 g carbohydrate, 2 g fiber, 3 g protein.

YOGURT MINI-MUFFINS

Each muffin is dipped in a honey-lemon mixture for extra flavor and moistness. Try this with other muffins or quick breads.

Nonstick spray coating
1 **cup all-purpose flour**
2 **tablespoons sugar**
¾ **teaspoon baking powder**
¼ **teaspoon baking soda**
¼ **teaspoon salt**
1 **slightly beaten egg white**
½ **cup plain nonfat yogurt**
2 **tablespoons cooking oil**
1 **tablespoon honey**
1 **teaspoon lemon juice**

Spray eighteen 1¾-inch muffin cups with nonstick spray coating; set aside.

In a large bowl stir together flour, sugar, baking powder, baking soda, and salt. Make a well in the center of the dry ingredients. In a small bowl combine egg white, yogurt, and oil. Add yogurt mixture all at once to the dry ingredients. Stir just till moistened (batter will be lumpy). Fill muffin cups ¾ full. Bake in a 400° oven for 10 to 12 minutes or till golden.

Meanwhile, for topping, in a small bowl combine honey and lemon juice. Set aside.

Cool muffins in pan on rack for 5 minutes; then remove muffins to rack. Dip tops of muffins in honey mixture. Serve warm. Makes 18.

Nutrition Information Per Muffin:
58 calories, 2 g total fat, 0 g saturated fat, 0 mg cholesterol, 57 mg sodium, 9 g carbohydrate, 0 g fiber, 2 g protein.

COFFEE CAKES AT THEIR BEST

This classic sweet bread is right at home in a healthy household thanks to our quick, low-fat versions. So help them taste their best by serving them warm. To reach that "just-right-for-eating" stage, let your coffee cake cool for 20 to 30 minutes before cutting and serving. If you can't wait that long, then give it a quick chill in your refrigerator for 5 to 10 minutes. Take advantage of leftovers for tomorrow's breakfast or an afternoon tea by storing coffee cake in an airtight container at room temperature.

DELECTABLE DESSERTS

COCOA-BERRY SHORTCAKES

1 cup all-purpose flour
¼ cup unsweetened cocoa
    powder
¼ cup sugar
1 teaspoon baking powder
3 tablespoons margarine
⅔ cup skim milk
1 large ripe banana, peeled
    and cut into chunks
½ cup frozen reduced-calorie
    nondairy whipped
    topping, thawed
½ cup plain nonfat yogurt
1 teaspoon honey
    Dash ground nutmeg
3 cups fresh strawberries

In a large bowl stir together flour, cocoa powder, sugar, and baking powder. Cut in margarine till mixture resembles coarse crumbs. Make a well in the center; add skim milk all at once. Stir just till dough clings together.

Drop in equal portions onto a lightly greased baking sheet. Bake in a 450° oven for 8 to 10 minutes. Cool slightly on a wire rack.

Meanwhile, for banana cream, in a medium bowl mash banana with a fork till smooth. (You should have about ½ cup.) Add whipped topping, yogurt, honey, and nutmeg; stir till smooth. Reserve 6 berries for garnish; slice remaining berries.

To assemble, split cocoa biscuits in half crosswise. Set tops aside. Arrange strawberry slices on bottoms. Dollop about *2 tablespoons* of the banana cream mixture over sliced berries on each biscuit. Top with the biscuit tops. Dollop *1 tablespoon* of the remaining banana cream on top of each of the assembled shortcakes. Garnish with the reserved whole strawberries. Makes 6 servings.

Nutrition Information Per Serving:
247 calories, 8 g total fat, 1 g saturated fat, 1 mg cholesterol, 104 mg sodium, 40 g carbohydrate, 3 g fiber, 6 g protein.

The rich-tasting banana cream filling for this recipe would also make a tasty dip for a variety of fresh fruit.

LIME-GINGER MOUSSE WITH BLACKBERRY SAUCE

Instead of scooping out each serving, you could serve this mousse in slices. Simply line the loaf pan with foil before adding the mousse mixture. Then lift out the frozen mousse using the foil, remove the foil, and cut into 8 slices.

MAKE AHEAD

1 cup evaporated skim milk
½ cup water
1 envelope unflavored gelatin
1 to 2 teaspoons grated fresh gingerroot
2 cups frozen blackberries
1 cup sugar
2 tablespoons crème de cassis (optional)
1 teaspoon finely shredded lime peel
⅓ cup lime juice, chilled
2 drops green food coloring (optional)

Pour evaporated milk into a large bowl; freeze for 10 to 15 minutes or till the milk becomes icy around the edges.

Meanwhile, in a small saucepan combine water and gelatin; let stand 5 minutes to soften. Add gingerroot. Bring mixture to boiling. Cook and stir till gelatin dissolves. Cool slightly.

Meanwhile, for sauce, place blackberries in a microwave-safe medium bowl. Micro-cook on 100% power (high) for 1½ minutes or till thawed, stirring once (or thaw berries overnight in the refrigerator). *Do not* drain. Press berries through a sieve, discarding solids. Stir in ¼ *cup* of the sugar and, if desired, crème de cassis. Cover and chill till serving time.

Beat icy evaporated milk on high speed of electric mixer to soft peaks. Add gelatin mixture in a thin stream to beaten evaporated milk, beating constantly. Gradually add remaining sugar, lime peel, lime juice, and food coloring (if desired), beating till the mixture becomes stiff enough to mound.

Transfer mixture to an 8x4x3-inch loaf pan. Cover and freeze several hours or till firm. To serve, scrape across the top of mousse with an ice cream scoop and mound into dessert dishes. Serve with chilled blackberry sauce. Makes 8 servings.

Nutrition Information Per Serving: 145 calories, 0 g total fat, 0 g saturated fat, 1 mg cholesterol, 39 mg sodium, 35 g carbohydrate, 2 g fiber, 4 g protein.

RICOTTA FRUIT DIP

⅓ cup fat-free ricotta cheese
2 tablespoons powdered sugar
1 tablespoon orange juice
½ teaspoon vanilla
⅓ cup vanilla *or* peach low-fat
  yogurt
2 cups strawberries, melon
  balls, *and/or* other cut-up
  fruit

In a blender container or food processor bowl combine the ricotta cheese, powdered sugar, orange juice, and vanilla. Cover and blend or process till smooth. Stir into the yogurt.

If desired, cover and chill up to 24 hours. Serve with berries, melon, and other fruit. Makes 4 servings.

Cut-up melon, pineapple, and other fruit in the produce section of your grocery store are great timesavers in this easy recipe.

MAKE AHEAD

Nutrition Information Per Serving:
73 calories, 1 g total fat, 0 g saturated fat, 3 mg cholesterol, 27 mg sodium, 14 g carbohydrate, 1 g fiber, 4 g protein.

SELECTING FRESH FRUITS

There's no better low-fat choice for dessert than fresh fruit. Choose the best you can find for the most after-dinner satisfaction. Here's how.

Fruits should be plump, tender, brightly colored, and heavy for their size (this indicates moistness). Avoid fruits with mold, mildew, bruises, cuts, or other blemishes.

To ripen apricots, plums, peaches, nectarines, pears, or tomatoes, place them in a paper bag and let stand at room temperature for a few days or till desired ripeness. Once the fruit is ripe, store in the refrigerator.

ENGLISH SUMMER FRUIT PUDDING

To make this crowd-sized dessert even prettier at serving time, reserve some whole fresh berries and sprinke them over the low-fat yogurt.

MAKE AHEAD

1 **purchased angel food cake, cut into ½-inch thick slices and crusts removed (about 1 pound)**
⅓ **cup orange juice *or* white grape juice**
¼ **cup sugar**
4 **cups fresh raspberries**
2 **cups peeled and chopped ripe peaches**
  Fresh raspberries (optional)
  Vanilla low-fat yogurt (optional)

Arrange about three-fourths of the cake slices on bottom and sides of an 8-cup souffle dish, overlapping or cutting pieces to fit; set aside.

In a small saucepan stir together orange or grape juice and sugar. Heat just till sugar dissolves. Remove from heat. Stir in 4 cups raspberries and peaches. Pour fruit mixture into cake-lined souffle dish. Cover with remaining cake slices. Cover top of dish with waxed paper. Place a heavy plate atop dish. Weigh plate down with a heavy object such as a can of fruit or a pan. Chill overnight.

To serve, remove the weight, plate, and paper. Gently loosen edges with a thin-bladed knife. Invert onto serving plate. Garnish with additional raspberries and serve with yogurt, if desired. Makes 10 servings.

Nutrition Information Per Serving: 182 calories, 0 g total fat, 0 g saturated fat, 0 mg cholesterol, 122 mg sodium, 42 g carbohydrate, 3 g fiber, 4 g protein.

BANANA YOGURT SHERBET WITH CHOCOLATE SYRUP

This "cool" dessert has a creamy texture and smooth mouthfeel thanks to the banana. Be sure to peel the bananas before freezing them since they are hard to peel once frozen.

MAKE AHEAD

1½ **pounds ripe bananas**
   (about 4 to 5 medium)
1 **8-ounce carton plain nonfat**
   yogurt
2 **tablespoons honey**
1 **tablespoon lemon juice**
2 **teaspoons vanilla**
   Dash ground nutmeg
⅓ **cup chocolate-flavored syrup**

Peel bananas; cut into chunks. Place banana chunks in plastic freezer bags. Freeze for 2 hours or till solid.

Remove bananas from freezer; separate chunks. In a blender container or food processor bowl combine yogurt, honey, lemon juice, vanilla, and nutmeg. Add frozen bananas. Cover and blend or process about 3 minutes or till the mixture is smooth. Transfer banana mixture to a deep stainless steel bowl. Cover and freeze for 6 hours or till firm.

Allow sherbet to stand for 5 minutes at room temperature. To serve, scrape across top of sherbet with an ice cream scoop and mound into dessert dishes. Top each serving with about *2 teaspoons* of the chocolate syrup. Makes 7 servings.

Nutrition Information Per Serving:
133 calories, 1 g total fat, 0 g saturated fat, 1 mg cholesterol, 33 mg sodium, 32 g carbohydrate, 1 g fiber, 3 g protein.

ORANGES WITH GINGERSNAPS AND DRIED CHERRIES

4 **medium oranges**
Orange juice
1 **tablespoon honey**
1 **teaspoon cornstarch**
⅓ **cup dried cherries**
2 **gingersnap cookies** *or*
4 **vanilla wafers,**
coarsely crumbled

Working over a small bowl to catch juices, peel and section oranges. Add enough additional orange juice to equal ½ cup juice. Place orange segments on paper toweling to drain.

For cherry sauce, in a small saucepan combine orange juice, honey and cornstarch. Add cher-ries. Cook and stir till thickened and bubbly. Cook and stir for 2 minutes more.

To serve, arrange orange segments on individual dessert plates. Spoon cherry sauce over orange segments. Top with the crumbled cookies. Makes 4 servings.

Nutrition Information Per Serving:
109 calories, 0 g total fat, 0 g saturated fat, 0 mg cholesterol, 21 mg sodium, 26 g carbohydrate, 2 g fiber, 1 g protein.

If you can't locate dried cherries, then use dried cranberries, dried blueberries, or mixed dried fruit bits.

THE SCOOP ON FROZEN DESSERTS

The freezer section is brimming with a variety of ice-cream-like treats in a multitude of tempting flavors. Which one is best for a healthy diet? Here's the scoop to help you decide.

Ice cream: This silky smooth dessert is made with at least 10 percent milk fat by law. And watch out because some of the premium ice creams go well beyond the 10 percent mark.

Ice milk: It's a kissing cousin to ice cream in flavor and texture but contains a lower fat content (2 to 7 percent milk fat).

Frozen yogurt: Currently there are no federal standards for this product which means you'd better read the label to find out its nutrition profile. Some brands are similar to ice cream while others are more like ice milk.

Sherbet: This fruity dessert must contain between 1 and 2 percent milk fat by weight. To offset the tanginess from the fruits used, more sweetening is often added to sherbets.

FRUITED MERINGUE SHELLS

2 egg whites
½ teaspoon vanilla
    Several drops almond extract
    Dash cream of tartar
2 tablespoons sugar
1 tablespoon strawberry, red
    raspberry, orange, *or*
    apricot all-fruit spread
1 tablespoon orange juice
2 cups cut-up seasonal fresh
    fruit (such as strawberries,
    grapes, blueberries, cut-up
    melon, cut-up mango,
    and/or cut-up papaya)
1 cup vanilla-flavored ice milk

In a medium bowl combine egg whites, vanilla, almond extract, and cream of tartar. Beat on high speed till soft peaks form; gradually add sugar beating till stiff peaks form. Divide mixture evenly between four individual quiche dishes or 10-ounce custard cups. Spread to form a shell. Bake in a 400° oven for 5 to 7 minutes or till lightly brown and set. Cool on wire rack about 10 minutes.

Meanwhile, combine all-fruit spread and orange juice; toss with fruit. Spoon into meringue shells. Top with ice milk. Serve immediately. Makes 4 servings.

Nutrition Information Per Serving:
117 calories, 2 g total fat, 1 g saturated fat, 5 mg cholesterol, 55 mg sodium, 23 g carbohydrate, 2 g fiber, 4 g protein.

These fruit-filled meringue shells are a deliciously light ending to any meal. Since they don't store well, prepare them just before you plan to serve them.

215

PEACH AND CURRANT COMPOTE

For a special treat, spoon this fruity warm compote over a scoop of frozen vanilla yogurt.

⅓ **cup orange juice**
2 tablespoons currant jelly
   Dash ground nutmeg
3 cups sliced fresh *or* frozen peeled peaches
2 tablespoons dried currants
   Fresh mint leaves (optional)

In a medium saucepan combine orange juice, currant jelly, and nutmeg; stir in peaches and cur- rants. Bring to boiling; reduce heat. Cover and simmer for 5 to 8 minutes or till fruit is just tender.

Serve warm or let cool to room temperature. Garnish with fresh mint leaves, if desired. Makes 4 servings.

Nutrition Information Per Serving: 104 calories, 0 g total fat, 0 g saturated fat, 0 mg cholesterol, 2 mg sodium, 27 g carbohydrate, 3 g fiber, 1 g protein.

FRUITY WINTER BAKING

Just because it's the dead of winter doesn't mean that you can't enjoy a luscious fruit dessert like the ones sprinkled throughout this chapter. Simply buy frozen fruit and use our easy sub- stitution techniques listed below that were perfected in the Better Homes and Gardens® Test Kitchen.

● Buy unsweetened frozen fruit as a direct substitute for fresh fruit. Read the label to determine if the product you're buying has added sugar or sweeteners.

● If the recipe calls for chopped fresh fruit, then chop the fruit while it's still frozen and use it immediately. If the fruit thaws, the juices may discolor the batter.

● If there are large clumps of frozen fruit or ice crystals, place the frozen fruit in a colan- der and rinse with cold water to break up the fruit.

● For fruit pies, mix the frozen fruit with the sugar and thickener called for in the recipe. Let stand about 30 minutes or till a syrup forms, then fill the pastry shell. Bake the pie longer than a fresh fruit pie (about 25 to 30 minutes longer). To prevent overbrowning, cover the crust with foil during part of the baking.

● For fruit crisps, thaw the frozen fruit but do not drain. Mix the thawed fruit and juices as directed for fresh fruit in the recipe.

● For fruit cobblers, it is not necessary to thaw the fruit because it will thaw during the baking time.

CREAMY RICE PUDDING

⅓ **cup water**
⅓ **cup quick-cooking rice**
¼ **cup sugar**
4 **teaspoons cornstarch**
1½ **cups skim milk**
1 **beaten egg**
1 **teaspoon margarine**
1 **teaspoon vanilla**
¼ **cup raisins**

Bring water to boiling. Stir in rice. Cover; remove from heat. Let stand for 5 minutes.

Meanwhile, in a heavy medium saucepan combine sugar and cornstarch. Stir in milk. Cook and stir over medium heat till mixture is thickened and bubbly. Cook and stir for 2 minutes more. Remove from heat. Gradually stir about *1 cup* of the hot mixture into the beaten egg.

Return all of the egg mixture to the saucepan. Cook over medium-low heat till nearly bubbly, but *do not* boil. Remove from heat. Stir in margarine and vanilla. Stir in rice and raisins. Cover surface with clear plastic wrap. Cool slightly or chill for several hours. Serve the pudding warm or chill and serve cold. Makes 4 servings.

Another time, try this stove-top rice pudding with dried cherries, blueberries, cranberries, or mixed fruit bits in place of the raisins.

Nutrition Information Per Serving:
175 calories, 2 g total fat, 1 g saturated fat, 55 mg cholesterol, 77 mg sodium, 33 g carbohydrate, 1 g fiber, 6 g protein.

KIWI FRUIT AND BERRIES WITH GINGER SAUCE

To save time when you serve this refreshing dessert, stir together the frozen yogurt and ginger up to 24 hours in advance and store it in the freezer. At serving time, place a scoop of frozen yogurt mixture on top of the sliced fresh fruit and drizzle with chocolate.

1   cup vanilla frozen yogurt, softened
2   tablespoons finely chopped crystallized ginger
4   large kiwi fruit, peeled and cut into six slices
½   cup small strawberries, sliced
½   cup red raspberries
2   tablespoons semisweet chocolate pieces
1   teaspoon shortening

In a small mixing bowl combine frozen yogurt and the crystallized ginger. Stir till yogurt softens to a sauce. Spoon *2 tablespoons* of the yogurt mixture onto *each* of *four* dessert plates. On each plate, arrange kiwi and strawberry slices over yogurt mixture. Sprinkle with raspberries.

In a small saucepan heat chocolate pieces and shortening together over low heat, stirring constantly till melted. Drizzle chocolate in thin lines over fruit and yogurt mixture. Makes 4 servings.

Nutrition Information Per Serving:
187 calories, 5 g total fat, 2 g saturated fat, 1 mg cholesterol, 35 mg sodium, 34 g carbohydrate, 1 g fiber, 3 g protein.

SPICED CORNMEAL BISCOTTI

¼ **cup margarine**
¾ **cup all-purpose flour**
¼ **cup yellow cornmeal**
¼ **cup sugar**
1 **egg white**
¼ **teaspoon finely shredded lemon peel**
¼ **teaspoon vanilla**
⅛ **teaspoon salt**
⅛ **teaspoon ground cinnamon**
2 **tablespoons finely chopped hazelnuts**
  Fresh raspberries (optional)

In a large bowl beat the margarine with an electric mixer on medium to high speed for 30 seconds. Add about *half* of the flour, cornmeal, sugar, egg white, lemon peel, vanilla, salt, and cinnamon. Beat till thoroughly combined. Beat or stir in remaining flour. Stir in the hazelnuts.

Shape the dough into 24 fingers, about 2½ inches long. Place on an ungreased baking sheet. Bake in a 375° oven about 10 minutes or till bottoms are golden. Remove cookies from baking sheet; cool on a wire rack. Serve with fresh raspberries, if desired. Makes about 24 cookies.

Nutrition Information Per Biscotti:
48 calories, 2 g total fat, 0 g saturated fat, 0 mg cholesterol, 37 mg sodium, 6 g carbohydrate, 0 g fiber, 1 g protein.

To divide the dough evenly, place dough on clear plastic wrap and use a rolling pin to flatten to a ¾-inch rectangle. Then remove the plastic wrap and cut the dough into 24 pieces.

MAKE AHEAD

FRUIT-SAUCED CAKE

This cholesterol-free white cake tastes equally delicious with cut-up seasonal fresh fruit. Sweeten the fruit with a little sugar, if desired.

Nonstick spray coating
1⅓ cups all-purpose flour
2 teaspoons baking powder
⅛ teaspoon ground nutmeg *or*
1 teaspoon finely shredded orange peel
¼ cup margarine
½ cup sugar
⅔ cup skim milk
2 egg whites
¼ cup sugar
½ teaspoon finely shredded orange peel
¼ cup orange juice
1 tablespoon cornstarch
1 10-ounce package frozen fruit in light syrup, thawed (red raspberries, strawberries, *or* mixed fruit)

Spray an 8x1½-inch round baking pan with nonstick spray coating. Sprinkle lightly with flour; shake out the excess flour; set aside.

Stir together the flour, baking powder, and nutmeg or the 1 teaspoon orange peel. Set the flour mixture aside.

In a large bowl beat margarine with an electric mixer on medium speed about 30 seconds. Add ½ cup sugar and beat till well combined. Alternately add the flour mixture and milk to the creamed mixture, beating on low to medium speed after each addition just till combined.

Wash and dry beaters. In a small bowl beat egg whites till soft peaks form (tips curl). Gradually add ¼ cup sugar, beating till stiff peaks form (tips stand straight). Gently fold egg white mixture into flour mixture. Spoon batter into prepared pan.

Bake in a 350° oven for 25 to 30 minutes or till a toothpick inserted near the center comes out clean. Cool cake in pan on a wire rack for 5 minutes. Remove the cake from pan. Cool completely on rack.

Meanwhile, for sauce, in a saucepan combine ½ teaspoon orange peel, orange juice, and cornstarch. Stir in thawed fruit. Cook and stir till thickened and bubbly. Cook and stir for 2 minutes more. Remove from heat; cool slightly. Serve slightly warm over cake or cover and chill and serve cool. Makes 8 servings.

Nutrition Information Per Serving:
235 calories, 6 g total fat, 1 g saturated fat, 0 mg cholesterol, 96 mg sodium, 42 g carbohydrate, 2 g fiber, 4 g protein.

TEMPTING
SNACKS

PITA WEDGES WITH BANANA SALSA

1 large ripe banana, peeled
   and diced *or* ¾ cup
   chopped fresh pineapple
1 medium nectarine, pitted
   and chopped (⅔ cup)
½ of a large green pepper,
   chopped (½ cup)
2 tablespoons snipped fresh
   cilantro *or* parsley
2 tablespoons lime juice

1 teaspoon brown sugar
   Toasted pita wedges from
   3 small pita bread rounds
   (see tip, page 231)

For banana salsa, in a medium bowl combine banana or pineapple, nectarine, green pepper, cilantro or parsley, lime juice, and brown sugar. Toss lightly to mix. Serve with toasted pita wedges. Makes 6 servings.

Nutrition Information Per Serving:
44 calories, 0 g total fat, 0 g saturated fat, 0 mg cholesterol, 19 mg sodium, 11 g carbohydrate, 1 g fiber, 1 g protein.

This sweet and tangy salsa makes a delicious dressing for cold cooked shrimp, too.

COTTAGE CHEESE AND DILL DIP

Serve this stir-together herb dip with a selection of ready-to-serve cut-up vegetables from your grocer's produce section.

MAKE AHEAD

1 cup low-fat cottage cheese
¼ cup reduced-calorie peppercorn ranch salad dressing
2 green onions, thinly sliced (2 tablespoons)
2 tablespoons finely chopped red *or* green sweet pepper
1 tablespoon finely snipped fresh dill *or* ¾ teaspoon dried dillweed
  Carrot strips, bias-sliced cucumber, *and/or* broccoli flowerets

In a blender container or food processor bowl combine cottage cheese and salad dressing. Cover; blend or process till smooth. Transfer to bowl; stir in green onion, pepper, and dill. Cover and chill up to 24 hours. Serve with carrot, cucumber, and/or broccoli. Makes about 1⅓ cups.

Nutrition Information Per 1 Tablespoon: 15 calories, 1 g total fat, 0 g saturated fat, 1 mg cholesterol, 74 mg sodium, 1 g carbohydrate, 0 g fiber, 2 g protein.

SMART SIPPING

Toasting friends and family with low- and no-alcohol beverages not only makes good sense, but it's easier than ever. Just check out the beverage aisle at your liquor or grocery store to discover the growing number of alcohol alternatives. Here's a quick rundown of what's available in most markets.

Nonalcoholic wines: They are fermented just like regular wine, then processed to remove the alcohol.

Low-alcohol wines: These wines undergo alcohol-removal processes similar to nonalcoholic wines, although some of the alcohol is left in.

Alcohol-free beer: Only malt beverages with no alcohol whatsoever may display this term. This product is typically made without traditional fermentation and instead gets its beer taste from added natural flavorings.

Nonalcoholic beer: Although the label suggests that these are free of alcohol, by law they must contain less than 0.5 percent alcohol. And don't look for the word beer on the label. They are called malt beverage, cereal beverage, or near beer. Brewers use several methods to make this product. Some rely on fermentation like regular beer and others do not.

Light beer: This term is not defined by law but generally refers to beer with about half the calories of regular beer. This does not mean half the alcohol content. Different brands vary in the amount of alcohol they contain.

GARDEN QUESADILLAS

2   **small green** *or* **red sweet peppers, cut into thin strips**
1   **small red onion, cut into thin, 1-inch long strips**
2   **teaspoons olive oil** *or* **cooking oil**
½   **teaspoon ground cumin**
½   **teaspoon chili powder**
2   **tablespoons snipped cilantro** *or* **parsley**
⅓   **cup fat-free cream cheese product**
5   **6- to 7-inch flour tortillas**

In a large nonstick skillet cook peppers and onion in *1 teaspoon* of the oil for 3 to 5 minutes or till crisp-tender. Stir in cumin and chili powder. Cook and stir for 1 minute more. Stir in snipped cilantro or parsley; set aside.

Meanwhile, spread cream cheese over half of one side of each tortilla. Top with pepper mixture. Fold tortilla in half over peppers, pressing gently.

Place tortillas on ungreased baking sheet. Brush tortillas with remaining oil. Bake in a 425° oven for 5 minutes. Cut each quesadilla into 4 wedges. Serve warm. Makes 10 servings.

Nutrition Information Per Serving:
60 calories, 2 g total fat, 0 g saturated fat, 1 mg cholesterol, 102 mg sodium, 9 g carbohydrate, 1 g fiber, 3 g protein.

You'll find specks of green or red sweet peppers and red onion peeking out from these Southwest-seasoned appetizers.

CURRIED CRAB DIP

2 **8-ounce containers plain nonfat yogurt (without gelatin)**

1 **cup cooked crabmeat (6 ounces)**

2 **green onions, chopped (2 tablespoons)**

1 **to 2 tablespoons chutney**

1 **teaspoon curry powder**

¼ **teaspoon salt**
   Dash ground red pepper
   Sliced green onion (optional)
   Low-fat crackers, carrot strips, *and/or* cucumber slices

Line a large strainer with a double thickness of cheesecloth and place it over a medium bowl. Spoon the yogurt into the strainer. Cover and refrigerate overnight. Discard any liquid in the bowl; wash and dry the bowl.

In the bowl combine drained yogurt, crabmeat, green onion, chutney, curry powder, salt, and red pepper. Cover and chill till serving time or up to 4 hours.

Place crab dip in a serving bowl. Garnish with additional green onion, if desired. Serve with carrots, cucumber, or crackers. Makes about 2 cups.

Nutrition Information Per 1 Tablespoon: 17 calories, 0 g total fat, 0 g saturated fat, 5 mg cholesterol, 45 mg sodium, 2 g carbohydrate, 0 g fiber, 2 g protein.

For a thick, creamy texture, be sure to drain the plain yogurt overnight in your refrigerator.

MAKE AHEAD

CRISP GARLIC POTATO SKINS

Here's a low-fat, low-sodium version of a popular restaurant-style appetizer.

MAKE AHEAD

2 **large baking potatoes**
2 **teaspoons olive oil** *or* **cooking oil**
2 **tomatoes, seeded and chopped**
¼ **teaspoon dried basil, crushed**
⅛ **teaspoon garlic powder**
2 **teaspoons grated Parmesan cheese**

One day or several hours ahead, prick potatoes with a fork. Bake in a 425° oven for 40 to 50 minutes or till tender. Cool. Wrap and store in refrigerator.

At serving time, cut baking potatoes into quarters. Scoop out the insides (reserve for another use), leaving ½-inch-thick shells.

Lightly brush both sides of potato skins with olive oil. Place, cut side up, on a large baking sheet. Bake in a 425° oven about 15 minutes or till crisp.

Meanwhile, in a small bowl combine the chopped tomatoes, basil, and garlic powder. Spoon some of the tomato mixture into each potato quarter. Sprinkle with Parmesan cheese. Bake for 2 to 3 minutes more or till heated through. Makes 4 servings.

Nutrition Information Per Serving:
107 calories, 3 g total fat, 1 g saturated fat, 1 mg cholesterol, 27 mg sodium, 19 g carbohydrate, 0 g fiber, 2 g protein.

JUICY READING

If you've read a fruit beverage label lately, most likely you saw the words such as juice blend, fruit drink, or natural. The confusion comes from a lack of government standards for these sippers, so the amount of actual fruit juice used in these drinks differs from brand to brand. A little sleuthing reveals the meaning behind the following terms.

● 100 percent juice: This is a beverage made with pure fruit juice and your best choice for a healthy thirst-quencher.

● 100 percent natural: This means the product contains no juice or as little as 10 percent. The remaining ingredients may be water, sweeteners, and flavors.

● Fruit juice blend, punch, beverage, or sparkler: A drink with one of these labels has some pure fruit juice, but sweeteners, water, and flavors may be added. The amount of pure fruit juice varies from brand to brand.

● Fruit flavored: Chances are this product contains no juice and mostly sugar. By law, powdered drinks must bear this label.

SWEET PEPPER SALSA WITH TOAST MEDALLIONS

2   medium red sweet peppers, chopped
1   medium yellow *or* green sweet pepper, chopped
¼   cup finely chopped onion
2   teaspoons snipped fresh basil *or* ½ teaspoon dried basil, crushed
2   teaspoons snipped fresh oregano *or* ½ teaspoon dried oregano, crushed
¼   teaspoon ground pepper
1   large clove garlic, minced
1   teaspoon olive oil *or* cooking oil
1   small tomato, chopped
1   tablespoon lemon juice
1   8-ounce loaf baguette-style French bread

For salsa, in a large skillet cook red pepper, yellow or green pepper, onion, basil, oregano, pepper, and garlic in hot oil for 3 to 5 minutes or till crisp-tender. Stir in tomato and lemon juice. Set aside.

For toast medallions, bias-slice bread into 24 pieces, about ½-inch thick. Arrange on baking sheet. Broil 5 to 6 inches from heat for 2 to 3 minutes or till lightly toasted. Turn bread over and broil 2 to 3 minutes more. Serve salsa with toast medallions. Makes about 24 servings.

Nutrition Information Per Serving:
29 calories, 0 g total fat, 0 g saturated fat, 0 mg cholesterol, 52 mg sodium, 5 g carbohydrate, 0 g fiber, 1 g protein.

Another time, serve this refreshing salsa with toasted tortilla or pita chips (See tip below.)

A CHIP OFF THE NEW BLOCK

Forget the old standby greasy chips that once invaded your snacktray. Chips made in minutes from tortillas or pita bread are not only novel but are low in fat and salt.

To prepare a batch of these new chips, stack flour or corn tortillas and cut into 6 or 8 wedges using a sharp knife or kitchen shears. For pita bread rounds, cut each bread in half horizontally, then stack and cut them into 6 or 8 wedges. Place tortilla or pita wedges in a single layer on an ungreased baking sheet. Bake, uncovered, in a 350° oven for 10 to 12 minutes or till crisp.

You can save any leftovers by storing them in an airtight container at room temperature for several days.

DRIED TOMATO CROSTINI

12 **dried tomato halves**
   (dry pack)
¼ **cup boiling water**
 2 **tablespoons balsamic** *or*
   red wine vinegar
 1 **ripe medium tomato, peeled,**
   seeded, and chopped
   (½ cup)
¼ **cup finely chopped red onion**
 4 **pitted ripe olives, minced**
   (optional)
 1 **tablespoon olive oil** *or*
   cooking oil
1½ **teaspoons snipped parsley**
 1 **clove garlic, minced**
½ **teaspoon capers, drained and**
   chopped
   Cracked black pepper
 1 **8-ounce loaf baguette-style**
   French bread

In a small bowl combine dried tomatoes, boiling water, and vinegar. Let stand for 15 to 20 minutes to soften tomatoes. Drain; discard liquid. Cut dried tomatoes into thin strips; return to bowl. Stir in ripe tomato, onion, olives (if desired), oil, parsley, garlic, and capers. Season with pepper.

Bias-slice the bread into 24 pieces about ½ inch thick. Place bread slices on a baking sheet. Bake in a 350° oven for 3 to 5 minutes or till light brown. Turn bread over; bake for 3 to 5 minutes more or till light brown.

Serve tomato mixture with toasted bread. Makes 24 servings.

Nutrition Information Per Serving:
38 calories, 1 g total fat, 0 g saturated fat, 0 mg cholesterol, 55 mg sodium, 6 g carbohydrate, 0 g fiber, 1 g protein.

Crostini is Italian for croutons or small pieces of toast. This easy version is topped with a full-flavored dried tomato spread and cheese.

Index

Nutrition Analysis

Keep track of your daily nutrition needs by using the information we provide at the end of each recipe. We've analyzed the nutrition content of each recipe serving for you. When a recipe gives an ingredient substitution, we used the first choice in the analysis. If it makes a range of servings (such as 4 to 6), we used the smallest number. Ingredients listed as optional weren't included in the calculations.

D-F

Index

Metric Cooking Hints

By making a few conversions, cooks in Australia, Canada, and the United Kingdom can use the recipes in Better Homes and Gardens® *Quick, Healthy and Delicious Cooking* with confidence. The charts on this page provide a guide for converting measurements from the U.S. customary system, which is used throughout this book, to the imperial and metric systems. There also is a conversion table for oven temperatures to accommodate the differences in oven calibrations.

Volume and Weight: Americans traditionally use cup measures for liquid and solid ingredients. The chart (top right) shows the approximate imperial and metric equivalents. If you are accustomed to weighing solid ingredients, here are some helpful approximate equivalents.
● 1 cup butter, caster sugar, or rice = 8 ounces = about 250 grams
● 1 cup flour = 4 ounces = about 125 grams
● 1 cup icing sugar = 5 ounces = about 150 grams
  Spoon measures are used for smaller amounts of ingredients. Although the size of the tablespoon varies slightly among countries, for practical purposes and for recipes in this book, a straight substitution is all that's necessary.
  Measurements made using cups or spoons should always be level, unless stated otherwise.

Product Differences: Most of the ingredients called for in the recipes in this book are available in English-speaking countries. However, some are known by different names. Here are some common American ingredients and their possible counterparts:
● Sugar is granulated or caster sugar.
● Powdered sugar is icing sugar.
● All-purpose flour is plain household flour or white flour. When self-rising flour is used in place of all-purpose flour in a recipe that calls for leavening, omit the leavening agent (baking soda or baking powder) and salt.
● Light corn syrup is golden syrup.
● Cornstarch is cornflour.
● Baking soda is bicarbonate of soda.
● Vanilla is vanilla essence.

Useful Equivalents

⅛ teaspoon = 0.5ml
¼ teaspoon = 1ml
½ teaspoon = 2 ml
1 teaspoon = 5 ml
¼ cup = 2 fluid ounces = 50ml
⅓ cup = 3 fluid ounces = 75ml
½ cup = 4 fluid ounces = 125ml

⅔ cup = 5 fluid ounces = 150ml
¾ cup = 6 fluid ounces = 175ml
1 cup = 8 fluid ounces = 250ml
2 cups = 1 pint
2 pints = 1 litre
½ inch =1 centimetre
1 inch = 2 centimetres

Baking Pan Sizes

American	Metric
8x1½-inch round baking pan	20x4-centimetre sandwich or cake tin
9x1½-inch round baking pan	23x3.5-centimetre sandwich or cake
11x7x1½-inch baking pan	28x18x4-centimetre baking pan
13x9x2-inch baking pan	32.5x23x5-centimetre baking pan
2-quart rectangular baking dish	30x19x5-centimetre baking pan
15x10x2-inch baking pan	38x25.5x2.5-centimetre baking pan (Swiss roll tin)
9-inch pie plate	22x4- or 23x4-centimetre pie plate
7- or 8-inch springform pan	18- or 20-centimetre springform or loose-bottom cake tin
9x5x3-inch loaf pan	23x13x6-centimetre or 2-pound narrow loaf pan or paté tin
1½-quart casserole	1.5-litre casserole
2-quart casserole	2-litre casserole

Oven Temperature Equivalents

Farenheit Setting	Celsius Setting*	Gas Setting
300°F	150°C	Gas Mark 2
325°F	160°C	Gas Mark 3
350°F	180°C	Gas Mark 4
375°F	190°C	Gas Mark 5
400°F	200°C	Gas Mark 6
425°F	220°C	Gas Mark 7
450°F	230°C	Gas Mark 8
Broil		Grill

Electric and gas ovens may be calibrated using Celsius. However, increase the Celsius setting 10 to 20 degrees when cooking above 160°C with an electric oven. For convection or forced-air ovens (gas or electric), lower the temperature setting 10°C when cooking at all heat levels.